Madurai Days

A Bond Beyond Times

SUBRAMANIAN

INDIA • SINGAPORE • MALAYSIA

Notion Press Media Pvt Ltd

No. 50, Chettiyar Agaram Main Road,
Vanagaram, Chennai, Tamil Nadu – 600 095

First Published by Notion Press 2021
Copyright © Subramanian 2021
All Rights Reserved.

ISBN 978-1-68509-604-5

This book has been published with all efforts taken to make the material error-free after the consent of the author. However, the author and the publisher do not assume and hereby disclaim any liability to any party for any loss, damage, or disruption caused by errors or omissions, whether such errors or omissions result from negligence, accident, or any other cause.

While every effort has been made to avoid any mistake or omission, this publication is being sold on the condition and understanding that neither the author nor the publishers or printers would be liable in any manner to any person by reason of any mistake or omission in this publication or for any action taken or omitted to be taken or advice rendered or accepted on the basis of this work. For any defect in printing or binding the publishers will be liable only to replace the defective copy by another copy of this work then available.

Dedicated to my guru Prof. Dr. G. Baskaran and my uncle V. Baladhandayudham

CONTENTS

Acknowledgements 7
Foreword 9

Madurai Days 11
    1. Seasons in 1980s and 1990s 13
    2. Glimpses of the Early 1980s 17
    3. Spots 24
    4. Festivals 74
    5. Persons 83
    6. Full Stop 91

ACKNOWLEDGEMENTS

I am extremely grateful to my Parents, wife and son for their support and encouragement. My special thanks goes to Prof.R.Nedumaran and Prof.G.Baskaran for their backing. My heartfelt gratitude goes to my friends ShahulHameed, Prakash Jain, Manish J.Shah, Sanjeev Jain and all my JV friends. I thank my students who helped in typing and doing all the formatting. I would also thank the popular photographer, Maduraikaaran Karthikeyan for his help. My final thanks goes to Lord Muruga, without whose grace I would not have been able to expand the thin thread of inspiration into a full fledged book.

FOREWORD

The book is historical and also personal. It's modern way of interpreting historical text.

Though Mr. Subramanian admits "I am neither a historian nor a literarian", he is both and he relates what I experienced during the same time as a college student. His attempt is genuine as he has made it very clear that there were many voices earlier narrated Madurai, spanning its existence of thousands of years. Even there were novels written, placing the city as a background. But this book is a document of Subramanian's personal childhood, his family, his relatives' visit, the festive occasions, the busy atmosphere at the streets in and around the temple, the mixture of tradition and modernity, the temple, the people, the distinctive shops, the seasons, the culture and what not. He has written briefly about the city in a lucid and simple language covering a decade of events and felt the unchanging Madurai ambience, its exclusive and significant one. He is creative and also sometimes philosophic in his reading of the city's river and temple. The book carries a sense of readability and message as Mr. Subramanian presents his teacher quality in it – especially the anglicizing the Tamil words. In it, in some of the places, he has given the words the freedom of choosing their placement. It is interesting to read and experience the authorial voice on the city.

HEARTY CONGRATULATIONS AND ALL THE BEST,
Prof G. Baskaran,
Professor and Dean
School of English & Foreign Languages
Gandhigram Rural Institute (DTBU)
Gandhigram - 624302

MADURAI DAYS

A BOND BEYOND TIMES

SEASONS IN 1980S AND 1990S

A Lot of writers had dealt with Madurai in different periods and still the town is as young as it was thousands of years ago, for a town'sage is not historical but generational. Every time a new generation is born, their view of the town changes and my perception of Madurai is based on how I saw the place in the 1980s and 1990s. Though a lot of pages are getting added every year about the town, the outlooks of the authors are exceedingly different. My view about the town is very much different as I am neither a historian nor a thoroughbred literarian. The present work is just an attempt to share my experiences pertaining to this great town that was born with culture and one that brims with activity. If at all there is a place in Tamil Nadu that has undergone least changes in the past one century, it is none but this great temple city. Even the word 'city' is an anomaly, as it resists modernity with full force; it is more of a village. 'Past' lingers in every nook and corner of the town and NRIs who visit the town after few decades of absence would be surprised to find the similarity of the spots that they had seen in their young age. Such a town has to be introduced not through its monuments, not through its culture, not through the educational institutions, but through the omnipotent weather. The intense heat that is noticed in summer season is an all pervading one and throughout the year the sun dominates except for a couple of months that we call as the rainy and winter season. Rains in Madurai in 1980s and 1990s were copious and pleasant. The evenings of July and August then were often burdened with heavy clouds that failed not to drench the town. The post rain nights were dark without electricity, with the isolated drops dripping audibly along with the whistling mosquitoes that were innocent then. The frogs did croak and the smell of wet 'green' brought in a sullen, somber feeling to the inmates of the house. Likewise the month of October and November were damper and the town did not have any time to dry. There were intermittent rains. The tight sands, the black roads that expose the dried patches here and there, the half melted *cowdungs*, the fresh smell of rains and the stagnant waters are some of the scenes that still stand in one's memory now. More than the monsoonal rains, the innocence of the sun to come back in the east as if nothing had happened in the previous night is the most interesting part of the rain-sun episode. Though there are no sharp seasonal changes, still a resident of Madurai was ever conscious of the sun and the rain.

As mentioned earlier, the sun was unrelenting and people could be seen moving quite normally with the wet sweat hanging on their back along with a typical *Madurai odour*[1]. But people shied not from heat as their love was to jostle in the crowd. Summers were long and cruelthen, and even walls were expected to sweat. It was a time when Air-conditioners were sparse and ordinary middle class homes were happy with table fans. Nights were hot and the moaning fan often aggravated the heat by lunging out hot puffs of air. Our family followed certain techniques to overcome the summer heat and one method was to water wash the room after the sunset. It was believed by my mother then that the heat would evaporate leaving the floor fit enough to comfort the sleepers. We used to open up the windows with the hope that summer winds would provide succor. But despite the heat, summer has loads of memories. It was a vacation time for schools- sans coaching and special classes- and lots of relatives used to descend to my home to spend their holidays. It was also a time for my grandmother to prepare *Vadagams*[2] for the whole year. It involved

---

1   Smell caused by intense sweat
2   A type of sidedish that complements the lunch in south Tamil nadu

a raw technique and my mother and aunt used to prepare the flour mixture the previous evening, and the next morning, a white cloth will be spread in the terrace on which the paste will be planted on the cloth to dry. After two or three days, we will all join to removethe dried stricken portion from the cloth which would be collected in a jar and roasted during lunch time to make our dinner delicious. Thus, summer had its own charm and Madurai was not an alien to the hot weather. We had green trees that withstood the heat and the dry rivers were a normal scene for any onlooker, as waters were dirty with raw weeds choking the river bed, while thestray cows musing at the mossy smell and the stretched out clothes drying itself in the muddy portions of the river. Summer had its own set of festivals, of which the *Chithrai*[3] festival of Madurai had a great significance. No place in the world relished a festival as freely as the people of Madurai did. It was an occasion that was cherished by all religions and it is a living example of the true *Indianism*. A massive crowd descended fromthe nearby villages and the constant chinks of the anklets even during nights were part and parcel of the Madurai culture. We, as young boys used to watch these *Kallars*[4] who dress themselves like Lord Alagar. Lord Alagar is a sacred deity for the Madurai people and in the month of *Chithrai*, he used to leave his abode in Alagarkoil to attend his sister Meenakshi's marriage. But by the time he reaches the wedding spot, the marriage gets over and in a huff enters the overflowing river. The occasion brought in a lot of crowd,and it brought us a great pleasure. The sound of cuckoo echoed throughout the season. Our house in Gandhi nagar had a wide open verandah, and me along with my cousin used to sit there to watch the cuckoo singing from a location in the big tree with a black tail. Though the day and nights were hot, there were times

---

3   First calendar month of a Tamil new year
4   A predominant caste in South Tamil nadu. LordAlagar is said to have entered Madurai to watch Goddess Meenakshi marriage dressed like a Kallar.

when summer rains lashed at the town with great fury leaving all road knee deep in the water. But summer seasons went away with huff and puff paving way for the monsoonal winds. It was normal in Madurai to have pleasant winds with hanging cloud during the late May and early June. The weather was temporary, as the pleasant atmosphere prevailed not beyond few days. After this sudden spell of monsoonal pleasantness, the heat generally went down, though the sun was at his usual self. June was a time in which there were pleasant morning breeze. The weather used to get more severe in the late July and August as it becomes almost akin to second summer. A general relief comes only during the month of October and November. The rains were persistent and at times it continued for a week without any break. Roads were always malnourished in the town and the monsoon tore the black coat into pieces of gravel and *thar* fragments. Every road was left broken and stones were protruding from their positions to damage the vehicle tyres. Every time when there was rain, Madurai was flooded and it was a sort of curse as pedestrians always had to wade through the waters, which were mostly dirty as drainage waters were prompt to mix-up with the stagnant pools. But Madurai survives, as the people are used to the waterlogged roads and none of them complain about it. And finally winter was very perfect as it never played truant. Generally, the year ended with chillness, and the people of Madurai generally overreact to the sudden change in temperature. A lot of precautions will be taken, and even in the 1980s, the miniscule *Yezdi, Jawa* and *Rajdoot* bike riders used to wear sweaters though the chillness was emaciated. Thus the season was less extreme in nature and accordingly, the people's behaviors were also generally neutral.

GLIMPSES OF THE EARLY 1980S

1980s was a decade between the past and the present. Madurai too was at the cusp of transformation. It was a time when there was a sudden interest in the electronic gadgets, new tape recorders and cassettes were omnipresent and the love for music was at its height. 'National' brand was the most sought after one and the one 'speakered' tape recorder with buttons on the top and a mouth big enough to accept a cassette was seen everywhere. The green coloured Sony cassettes and unique TDK ones were very much on the roll. Ilayaraja was emerging as a musician and every song from his harmonium was a hit. Added to this was the Ceylon Radio that was more popular amongst us. We were basically living as joint family with my Grandfather, Grandmother, Uncle, Aunt and Cousins. My parents along with me and my sister were in a room just opposite to my Uncle's room. It was a big house, though an old one. The massive verandah was rectangle in shape and it jutted out into a standing spot from where one could look at the narrow road. It was often my practice then to lean on the parapet wall and watch the scenes on the road. There was a big Hall that was termed as *Pattalai*.⁵ I do not know the reasons for such a name, but we went on using the same name. It was again a rectangular one with windows at the far ends. There were also windows in between hall and verandah along with doors at two corners. A puja room was adjacent to the hall and next followed the dining hall that had two bedrooms on each side. The dark kitchen, full of soot, and waterless basin alsohad a cemented table like protrusion, on which the water

---

5   'Hall' in Tamil. It is a word used in parts of Tirunelveli

containers were placed. It was a time when Madurai suffered from extreme water shortage and the government came up with a road side pump scheme.

Madurai in 1980s had people who appeared to be hot headed, but innocent. They appear rough, but are generally soft. In 1980s, the society in Madurai was not very prosperous as more number of thatched houses were seen all over the city. Due to dwindling opportunities only a segment of the society was employed. There were people who called themselves as middle class and they were the ones who resided in rented houses. The poorer ones were certainly large in numbers compared to the twenty first century. I would like to speak about individuals of those days who could stand out as the representations of the times.

The first person who strikes my mind is the vegetable vendor who was a regular gate crasher to our house. She was moderate in height with typical Tamil features and the tattoo in her hand that had often made me wonder for the reasons. She had a towel which was rolled in a circular manner to cushion her curly head from the heavy brown basket. It was her habit to walk in the streets of Madurai to sell the vegetables. She seldom wore any footwear and was quite fluent in her walk. For years, she trudged on the roads with vegetables, but I think after 1989, she was out of action and the reasons are beyond assumption. She is one fine example to showcase the power of women in 1980s. It was a time when most of the husbands were either unemployed or under employed,and there are lots of instances to highlight the unemployment problem in those days. But still when we think of the people like 'Chellama', it is a heartening thing. I can very well statethat seldom had she quarreled with any of us,and this is the reason why I termed the people of Madurai as one who maintained the equanimity.

Rickshaws were the mode of transport for middle class people who were unable to go in bus or did not have a car. My rickshawwala or the *Annan*[6] as we used to call him was a tall guy in south Indian terms. He was dark, with uncombed hair and stingy beard. Mostly, he used to wear the same checked full hand shirt that was folded along with the Lungi. He was poor, and at that age when I used to go to school along with my friends, I admired him. I still remember him pedaling

---

6   A Tamil usage for elder brother

and sweating the bus dotted roads. There used to be times when he used to pull the rickshaw, and this was in traffic junctions and in some elevated places. Though we used to be silent in mornings, our return trip was different as we used to keep chatting with him and most of the chat was in form of questions. He used to answer patiently, and there was always a towel on his neck which he used to wipe the sweat. I have never seen him miss his duty and above all now when I think of him, I feel that I need to owe my survival to him. He not only took us safely, but also behaved in a refined manner. The gentleness in the person is an extraordinary virtue and today's generation need to learn a lot of things from a person like him. It was a time when auto-rickshaws were totally absent. The days of jingling of the rickshaw bells that hung from the hand bar with a rope is literally over, but the sudden excitement that the sound produced was electric. *Annan*'s behavior, and gentleness despite his poverty and illiteracy goes on to prove the virtue of 1980s society. People were gentler, and less rude than the present day generation.

Someone has to be in the line, and the very next person whom I would like to discuss about is a shop owner who resided just in the next street of ours. His name was Nagarajan, and he ran a provisional store which had all sundry items relating to a household. He signified the typical business man of Madurai. He was dark and fat, who I felt seldom thought anything other than money. He was very scrupulous in money matters, and my grandmother often used to scold me and my cousin sister for having account in his shop. The elder lady probably should have felt that this man was cheating us. But still I do admire his relentless workmanship, for I had never seen him sitting in the shop. His whole family used to work in the shop and they never had an employee, for all their work was shared amongst the family members. Every January, he and his family went on a pilgrimage to *Palani* by walk. Even now when I visit the street with nostalgic memories, I would find this man standing in his shop and I was surprised that he still has a cycle. Though he earns a lot, he never spent money and this is how atypical Madurai business man behaved in those days.

The reason why I dealt with these three personsis just to show how the lower middle class and poor class lived in the 1980s. They never complained and never cheated. Even if they did, the number of people who were involved in such activities was miniscule. It was a decade when innocence was still alive and it should be remembered that it was a period that did not have telephone, for it was arare commodity. There were telegraph offices with telephones and to speak with a distant relative one has to book a 'Trunk Call'. There were times when we waited for more than two hours to speak with our relatives in the nearby town. Death message and Appointment messages was brought in by the ominous telegrams. STD was a latter addition that probably eased the choked communication between families. But, the all weather blue coloured inland letters connected people of all nature. The arrival of Post man around 11am was a great sense of Joy and curiosity. In terms of enjoyment, I would say that the Peoples only entertainment in those days were theatres and so, the number of corrupt minds were less. Every morning during holidays, when I stand in my verandah, the first thing that struck my eyes is the marble players who used to dig small holes near the road and at least three to four guys used to play marbles. I don't remember them to be young boys, for I had even seen a grown up men with *lungis*[7] throwing the marbles. I had wondered in admiration, and I still remember their body language, which used to be akin to a typical base ball bowler who throws a ball at the batsman. Here the marble is thrown at the holes, and the game itself is confusing, for I had not understood it till now. The holes they make on the ground

---

7   A typical south Indian dress used predominantly by Tamils and Malayalees in India

is an interesting sight and they use their toe to smoothen the hole. Atleast six to eight holes would be there and the thrower would take aim with a forward bend that was often coupled with the lift of a leg. But these guys were spending their time quite easily and only now I do realize the reasons for the same. 1980s was a time of staggered unemployment, and Indian economy was in dire straits. Employment was not forthcoming, and most of the poorer ones were idle. *Mathichiyam* was a strange place near our home that had a lot of working class people. Its road was narrow, made of big sandstones and there was no space as density was a bit high here. Now, people call it as a dangerous spot, but in my boyhood days, I have often visited and explored the inner streets of this so called 'slum'. There used to be a *Pillayar*[8] temple under a tree and an old lady used to be selling mangoes and other types of eateries which were haunted by me and my sister. There used to be small dingy mud houses and parked bicycles with semi-naked old women probing the trespassers from their *thinnais*[9]. We had few friends in those quarters and they used to take us to ice companies. We used to go to buy ice candy as it was cheap there, we devoured the stuff knowing not what to buy next. The reason why I just recount this incident is to mainly highlight the lifestyle of those times. People were poor, people could be ruffians, but they never disturbed others in any way and Madurai was such a place. Death of an old person here was a literal celebration and there used to be a nightlong Oppari or lament. A lot of crackers were burst with dance to send the lifeless body to its grave. Such a place are not frequented by many and I doubt if I would allow my children to explore these places in the same way as I did in those days. There are innumerable instances of Madurai gentleness and it is one town where a small mishap to any traveler or bike rider would elicit prompt response. Unlike the curiosity ridden onlookers of the other

---

8   A Tamil name for Lord Ganesha
9   A place in front of the village homes used for relaxation .

towns, here the people were genuine in offering help. One other stark fact about Madurai is that the residents can never confined within the walls for a long time, for socialization was natural, and neighbors became relatives.

Thus both weather and people are very important and both are directly proportional to each other. The weather could have had its impact on the people of the town and their behavior, temper and proclaimed hard headed attitude might be related to the weather. Life in 1980s was raw and natural with people complementing with better behavior than the current times. The weather men may argue that it was a decade, when summer was less hot and October was wet. But treeswere large in numbers and Madurai is one place where trees were seldom cut. The same trees that I saw in my boyhood eyes still smile at my middle age. They are still green and dark, with tonnes of stories about people and their attitude.

SPOTS

As mentioned in the earlier pages, there should not be any historical angle to the spots as the discussion is purely a subjective one. Madurai had many interesting spots which may not have attained popularity, but engaged us in a curious manner.

One spot that strikes me instantly is the Madurai Railway junction and like every small child, I was so excited to visit the Madurai junction as trains were my special attractions. In those days, I remember accompanying my grandfather to the railway junction along with my brother and sister. If my memory is precise, the train used to start from the station at 7.30pm and the train I am speaking about is the proud Pandyan Express. It was our habit then to accompany our grandfather to the station and bid him good bye. He used to carry a beige suit case and bed roll with him and I was in-charge of the latter. It gave me a great excitement to enter the buzzingstation, where,the people were moving hither and thither. Every sound and smell made me happy and as we neared the train in platform no.1, there used to be a pleasant smell that hangs on my nostrils even now. Though I did not know then, I later come to know that it was a cleansing agent that was used in toilets. Our train was loaded with the smell and it gave a special thrill. The speciality of Pandiyan express was such that it was painted in green and was the only southern train that had cushion berth.

The trains that plied then like Nellai Express and Quilon Express used to have wooden berth that was considered to be a normal thing then. So, as a *Maduraian*, I was often proud with the Pandiyan Express. We used to search for the compartment and used to settle my grandfather in it. The train was a meter gauge one that hadnormal faded cream coloured mica with minute floral designs all around and the dull golden light in every coach. The floors used to be brownish red that was clean and neat. As a boy, I had a special joy to connect my foot with the floor of the train by removing the slippers. We used to sit in the train for sometime before moving out to say our goodbyes. The bell would ring and the green signal on our far right of the platform would propel the train to move slowly. But soon there would be agradual increase in speed and I always felt empty to see the last coach crossing me. The final 'X' mark down behind the last coach in yellow paint is still fresh with the boding of a loss. Every time,the train leaves, there used to be a sort of fish smell, which I came to know was from the caravan car. While returning out of the platform, a black coated staff would be strictly collecting platform tickets that used to be a small rectangular card. I had often dreamt in those days to travel in Pandiyan Express and my wish got fulfilled only in 12th year. Madurai railway station was neat and clean even then, and nothing has much changed except for some digital boards and tickets. The steel pillars, asbestos roofs, the space, the platforms and the parking lots are almost similar to what I had seen then. Of course, the crowds were less and the buzz was little. There were less number of shops in the platforms then and above all there was something solemn in the stage. The old TVS building just opposite to the railway junction, the tea shops, the trees, the rickshaws near the parking spot are all well encased in my memory. Even now, when I visit the junction at times, the same old memories keep smiling at me. In the early 1990s, there used to be juice shop inside the station, which we used to call it as an apple juice shop. This was a meeting point for me and my brother as both of us loved to drink the chilled apple essence and it became a habit. In fact there were even times in the late 1990s when I used to go to the junction to have this drink as people were saying that apple juice makes a man smart. The station did not see much change in 1990s, as it was time when broad gauge conversion was happening. Travel then in a train was a huge thing and was often preceded by a lot of preparations. The trains by now had undergone changes. Pandiyan Express was no more green, as it was in the usual brown as Indian trains were. The Vaigai Express was in its usual golden yellow and green. The late 1990s changed the color of these trains to blue and even now it is the color of most trains. In 1994-1995, I and my uncle used to visit the junction quite often and most of our visits were to receive guests during our family functions. During such times, we used to start at the wee hours, and around 3:30 am in the morning we used to park the vehicle and wait for the train to arrive. It was a pleasure to wait outside the station when it was totally deserted. There were living bodies sleeping in the floors here and there and the silence of the morning was really joyous. There were no birds in sight, but were somewhere in some trees with weak moanings. Likewise, the high rise focus lights were introduced in Madurai in that period, and we loved to watch the power of it in wonder. Usually, most part of Madurai was lit with the Russian sodium vapor orange light. It was the only light in the town along with sparse tube lights. The old junction is very much changed in terms of the crowd and in terms of the train. But otherwise, the junction has more past in it.

In the early 1980s there was a spot that has slowly vanished from the people's mind and it is the milk booth. In my boyhood days there was one at the left angle to my home in Azad Street. The booths were a blue box like structures and an in charge would sit to handover the milk bottles then. In those times, milk was supplied in glass bottles unlike the plastic covers that are being used in the present times. Being a boy just 7 years old, I was woken up for it at 5:30am in my room. It was a small room that accommodated four of us and through the parapet wall that projected, I saw the milk booth in the blush silent mornings: I was asked to walk to collect the milk bottle and with a card in my hand I reached the booth to get my bottle. The card was punched manually and I traversed the sleepy road to return back in triumph to my home. Milk booth had always given me a special feeling almost akin to hope. The main reason is that it gave us the first sign of morning and more over the milk van that used to come to deposit the bottles gave me a special comfort. Ten years later when we resided P&T nagar, there was milk booth just opposite to my house and it was always occupied by a couple during the nights. Since the milk van came in the early mornings, the employees used to wait for the arrival from previous night itself. Though the van's arrival was rather disturbing, it gave us secured feeling as nights were lonely and silent. The days of milk booth alone supplying the milk packets are gone and now as the population has seen massive expansion, every shop sell the packets for the needy. Thus in few years, this too would pass and there will be times when milk will be supplied through pipe connections.

In the previous pages, I had mentioned about the provisional store that was near my home and it was run by a family. This was a strange shop that was located in the Jawahar street, and it was dull when seen from outside as the owner was so parsimonious that he neither lit nor ventilated his shop. But a lot of sacks and every stand was filled with some or other items. There was also an overwhelming incense smell that mingled with spices and other stuff to give a mixture of fragrance that was welcoming in nature. The shop did not have any hardcore protection then, as it was a weak wooden door that protected the shop. But as I said earlier, the people of 1980s were better in terms of values and morals that there were fewer crimes. One stuff,that was very popular amongst the children in 1980s was the white *Soodamittai*[10] that was neatly arranged in a big transparent bottle fit enough to attract the small children who walk on the streets. The shopowners had a technique of attracting customers of which arranging the "Mittai" bottles in the front of the shop was one that pulled children who were generally moving with their parents. In those days, they had a wooden table with a draw in which the business money was collected. The table was not in theinterior part of the shop, but was generally at the very entrance. The shop also had a steel chair in which the proprietor usually sat during afternoons. The jute thread that was used for packing used to hang from an elevated hold and it was nice to see the owner pulling the edge of the rope every time to tie the sold stuff. Another sweet that was available in the shop was a type of milk sweet that was neatly folded in a paper pack. The interesting thing about it is that there used to be coins inside the pack and lucky people could use it to get another toffee. Those were the

---

10   A white mint toffee popular in 1980s. It was round in shape.

days when 5 paise, 10 paise, 20 paiseand 25 paise coins were available and with one rupee in hand we can get a whole lot of toffees and sweets. There was a time in late 1980s when a new bubble gum was introduced in India and it was "Big Fun". The product was green in colour, and often gave an indifferent smell, but every one of us loved to buy it just because others bought it. As we imitated the cricketers, it was a habit for boys like me to buy the green gum for chewing. I need to recount my experiences with shampoo and when it was introduced it was in small transparent pack. This was another stuff that was popular in the shop.

As boys, me and my brother never shied away from visiting different spots that were in and around Gandhi nagar, andmy brother was more venturesome as he went through the different routes and different spots. I remember the days when we used to visit the saloon shop near the Priya theatres. It was not far away from our home and we used to tread the silent roads expecting fewer crowds in the shop. Few cycles and carts used to cross us, and there was a lovely cart at the corner of the road in those days. The main road used to be buzzing with buses and cycles and we need to cross the road to walk towards the Priya theatre that was located at the left end of the road. The saloon shop was on the way, and there were a couple of shops nearby and it was our wont to sit on the spineless stool for a long time till we got our chance to cut our hair. Often the owner used to bypass us for elderly customers, but as young boys we were too patient then,for a longtime. The shop was painted white with a lot of flower like decoration on the glass panes. The door was always kept open and there were three chairs attended by three persons. All the technical items that were used by the hair technicians were in front of us and the fashion then was to have "step cut". I and my brother used to go for a step cut and every time when we came back from the shop, my grandfather never failed to chide us for the cut. The owner of the shop was a pious man who was in his white shirt and dhoti and he was non-stop in discussing things with his customers. Generally, all rude guys become very gentle in saloon shops. The owner was very sincere and had many photos of gods and goddesses. A stereo National tape recorder used to play the new songs and he performed his duties unassumingly. At times a boy used to bring tea for three men of the shop and the shophad a strange name. It was christened as "NesaRojavin Prince" and I did not care about the meaning of the title then. In the course of time, I and my brother separated as we grew up. I started searching for new shops and there were many popular saloon shops like Odean, Brucelee, Prince and et.al. The Odean shop was the farthest one as it was located near the Madurai government hospital. I attempted to expand my travel zone a bit slowly after getting used to the cycle that I bought in the year 1986. It was a red 18 inches 'Hero' cycle. The shop to which I rode was a modern one with cooler glass and a lot of seats. Fresh perfume smell was on the hang and the men who were in work were a bit smart and modern. It was here did I hear the term "shampoo bath" which was done prior to hair cut. The other shop "Bruce lee" was a quaint little shop that was few steps away from the present one. Thus at the age when I was getting conscious about my personality, these were the shops that attracted me. There were many styles during the period of which 'step-cut' was one and it was followed by "attack" style. This went on for some time till "punk" emerged which stayed for some years before vanishing into oblivion.

Our house was in Azad street and it had three portions with two houses at the ground floor and one at the first floor. We actually stayed in the latter that was quite expansive to accommodate three families that included my parents, my uncle family, grandparents with a big hall that opened into a room and dining hall. There were two rooms near the dining hall which was actually used by my family and my uncle's. There were parapet walls in both the rooms that opened into eastern and western direction. The backyard of the house was extensive and had a big neem tree shading a part of the sitout. It was a rectangular opening with kitchen corners. There was a stair case which took people to the terrace and near the terrace was one broad iron pillar. Instead of walls, the left side of the terrace had perforated walls with yellow paint. One thing that struck me about the terrace was that it was highly uneven and had often felt it weak and ready to crumble anytime. As a young boy in 1983, I used to spend time in the terrace by looking at the eagles in the skies. In fact, a lot of eagles were seen in the skies then and when questioned I got a reply that it is due to mass killings of Tamils in Sri Lanka. The floor of the terrace was black and rough in nature. The backyard of house was often filled neem seeds and small figs that fell quite softly on the tiled floors. Many a times, I have felt the sticky seeds along with the leaves. There were times when we used to play under the shade during summers and my sister used to make us adorn the familial roles. We have also tried to cook some stupid stuff with the aid of figs and innovative burner. Our interests had always been temporary, and at a particular point of time we worked hard to bring in mud from the road to plant table roses. We were exceedingly happy to see the floor shining with table roses. Every morning when I used to wake up, I rush to the small garden of ours which never failed to smile at me with itscolours. This backyard was everything for me, for I brushed and even bathed there. It was a time when water was scarce and the plastic buckets were unknown. I reminisce the days when I used to take bath from the steel bucket that was quite hard and heavy which is unseen today. The most interesting time was summer when we used to sit at the backyard as a whole, except for my grandparents. There were transistors which sometimes played songs at the night time. In this backyard,we have chatted many a times and have often breathed the essence of *Chithrai* moon. There were times when the moving lights of the circus were interestingly watched by us on the skies. But I don't remember of having watched any stars in the night skies. Either it was absent or it was very much present and shone in our minds, I know not. The slow summer breeze had often ruffled our minds and it was a practice for us to eat our supper *Neerthani*[11] under the skies. Since TV was absent in the early 1980s, we had ample leisure time without boredom. This was how the families spent their time and till sleep swept the younger ones, the members were with the nature. But everything changed with television as it tore families away from the nature.

But what we do during evenings and during other holidays? A question of this nature could be answered through the games that we play during our free time. Cricket was our first passion and I was longing to join some of the guys who used to play at the further corner of my street. Since our street was relatively calm and long with lots of houses without any vacant spots, and huge trees that enveloped the sunlight enabled us to play our games there. There was a building which was more like a business establishment and it was here that I started playing cricket. My first game was in tennis ball. But I started getting intensely passionate as I played almost in every moment of the boyhood. I got to play on Sundays and it was spent fully in the street and there were times especially during summer vacation, when we used to play matches in the medical college ground. We used to carry stumps and other accessories and walk through the Anna bus stand that was located just behind my home. Since the traffic was not as heavy as it is now, it was easy for us to cross the roads. In those days, there was an 'S' type road that took us to the ground from Gandhi nagar and *Mathichiyam*[12]. It was a busy road as all the town buses that come from the Goripalayam used to take right and move along the 'S' road to reach their destination. There were different pathways to the ground which was a massive space with one main pitch. There were

---

11   A type of liquid diet, used by Tamil people during summer months. Prepared by rice soaked in water.
12   A slum like locality near Gandhi nagar

steel fences, but we used to cross it either through some dexterous method or we took a circuitous route to go through the main gate. At times there were oppositions, as we were not allowed to use the ground. But often we never failed to play and the ball that was used was cork ball which was heavy. Since I and my brother were small, we often did not get chance to play and it was only after a long time we were members of the team. There used to be a temple and a tree which was used by all as the players' pavilion.

The matches were extremely serious and there were times when quarrels erupt due to the game of cricket. Amongst us there were people like *Shiva* and *Kumar* who were hyper active and used to climb the trees and jump over the compound walls into the medical college hostel. Often, when the matches were over, it would be late evening and we used to rush to home with thirst and hunger. There were no mineral waters then, and me and my brother often quenched our thirst by dipping the tumblers in a big vessel which was called *Paanai*[13] in Tamil. In ground, sometimes there came ice vendors who sold *Kuchi*[14] ice to most of us at exorbitantly cheap price. A lot of matches were played in the above slated ground and during holidays, there used to be huge crowds with atleast 10 or 12 teams playing with each other. It is sad that the famous medical college ground in Madurai is no more as the grave digger have dug deep to raise the scepter of buildings on it. Whenever I cross the ground, I often turn to the spot where the ground was there to find hospitals and other heavy buildings.

Cricket continued in the 1990s as well, though in a smaller ground in P&T nagar, Madurai. It was an association ground and here it was a different ball game. I was alone here as my brother had shifted to another place and there were no full fledged matches as the

---

13   A big vessel container used for storage of water
14   Ice that is frozen on a stick

guys here often preferred to play with Tennis balls, still, there were intense matches and the bondage here was very less compared to the Gandhinagar team. After college under graduation times, there was a pause in cricket and I was spending most of my time in other pursuits. Now, I watch the ground being converted into a park, where people keep rounding on and on. Thus cricketing passion was so great and I had a wonderful time with my mates playing in different grounds.

Watching cricket was as passionate as playing cricket, but it all happened only after the entry of television into our home. Till Indira Gandhi died, no one ever thought of buying a Television, as most of the Indian middle class people saw it was an item of luxury. The sad day is still fresh in my memory. I was in my fourth standard seated in a corner of a white painted room with grey window. My teacher Mrs. Jayalakshmi was teaching us History, but suddenly anattendant entered to tell something to the teacher. She immediately went out, and there was a great buzz as teachers were moving here and there, with one lady using her transistor. My elderly teachers were able to understand through various sources that the dynamic Indian Prime Minister Shrimati. Indira Gandhi was assassinated. As a young boy, I was not so perturbed, but was a little bit happy to return to my home. Luckily my uncle had come with few children of the neighborhood on the car and took me to my home. The roads were empty and only one house in the vicinity had television then. It was our opposite house and they were our family friends. The head of the family was a retired judge and we barged to watch the last rites of Indira Gandhi. The elders were speaking about her Aryan nose and we saw the children of Rajiv Gandhi in extreme sorrow. Finally the pyre was lit and we all had to come back. It was great feelings for me to have an encounter with TV for the first time. I was literally overjoyed and after returning to my home started pestering my father to buy a TV. In twenty days from the death of late Indira Gandhi, we bought our first TV in a shop owned by our family friend known as 'TV traders'.

I still remember the date and it was November 19, 1984, the day was ironically Indira Gandhi's birthday. We brought the TV in our Ambassador car that accommodated the big Solidaire box and the antenna along with few rods arrived in a tricycle. The whole night we were eager about the Television and the next morning around 11'o' clock the TV mechanics came and fitted the antennas with booster. The TV had its own booster and it was switched on and there were some Hindi programmes. There were two antennas then, a bigger one was in the direction of Kodaikanal station, and the smaller one was towards Colombo. But somehow, the TV was switched on in the evenings to watch the stale Hindi programmes. My father watched the English news of Doordarshan with popular readers like Rita Khanna and KalpanaIyer and so on colouring the gadget. There were good serials that were telecast and we guys watched without understanding the language. "Hum Log" was a popular soap along with "Ramayan" on Sundays. There were "Chitrahars" on Wednesday and Friday and we often thought that Friday "Chitrahar" was of much better quality as it was from Delhi Station while Wednesday was from Bombay Station. Though Hindi was the language of TV in India, we had our succor through Rupavahini. Though Madurai was far away, we received signal after 7pm. There were times when watching Tamil movies was a rare phenomenon and Rupavahini satiated the desire. I will not forget the day on which me and my father were trying to watch a Tamil movie by name "Motor SundaramPillai". It was a nice movie, but we were not blessed to watch movie to its end as there were problems with the signal. The Sundays were quite full in Madurai as most of the households were busy watching "Ramayan" serial eventhough it was in the language of Hindi. No one cared about understanding the serial, for they all knew the story. It was almost a sort of reenactment in TV. At 1.30 pm there was a news for the impaired in Doordarshan and we used to watch a fat lady squeezing and stretching her fingers for the physically challenged. This was followed by the regional movie slot and the the channel used to telecast award winning tamil movies. I remember to have watched movies like *Raja Paarvai, Kappalotiya Tamizhan and SivagangaiSeemai* more than once as the same movies were repeated. This was how the days in Madurai in 1980s were spent. There were many programmes, and slowly people were losing themselves in Television which eventually disrupted the old way of Life. India – Pakistan matches were so popular then, but the strong state of affairs was that India never won against Pakistan except occasionally. Matches took place very often in Sharjah and we all would watch with great expectation. Players like Srikanth, Gavaskar, Ravi Shastri, Vengsarkar were all individually popular ones, but when it came to Pakistan all this people struggled. We in our home have always felt that Ravi Shastri was a player of least use, but he held on to the team for a long time probably for unknown reasons. So, TV not only brought pleasure, but often made us sad too.

Here, I need to share a few words about my school SDH. Jain Vidyalaya that was located in Sellur area in Madurai. In the earlier part of my school days, I reached the school in Rickshaws for there were no school buses and vans. My school was run by Gujarati Samaj and it was considered to be a costly school. Despite its poshness, it was located in a place that was strange as there was a big gutter that was running like a river. It was a big one, but it did not add negativity to the school. It had two gates, of which the front gate was for entry in the morning and the side gate was for exit. There were large trees of which the big badam tree is even now fresh in my memory. The big leaves of these trees used to float in mud and at times the fruit falls on the ground. I have often felt like eating the fruit but felt so self conscious to pick it up from the ground. There were see-saws and merry go roundsthat was a fun then. There was an office at the entry point of the building on the right side after which the classrooms were located. My kinder garten days were spent in a hall that was then called as Auditorium and it was here that we sat on round tables and my teacher L. Rozario taught us rhymes and things that could be termed as knowledge. A lot of outdoor activities were conducted and we owe a lot to this great teacher.

The school was in a busy location that it was surrounded by buildings and busy roads were full of nonstop traffic. There were trees and sit-outs on the right side of the sole building and usually this was the spot we used for viling away our time. A gooseberry tree, with small size berries on it was always a source of attraction for me and there were days when I used to shake the tree along with my friend to loosen the tree's grip on the berries. We used to collect few stuff that falls on the ground and used to taste the bitter berries with great fondness. But overall the texture of sand was such that it was a bit hard and it was uneven as in few spots there were more sand, while in some places there was no sand. Many a times we ran to fall on those places to bruise our knees. The mixture of blood and sand often gave us pleasure then and we never cared about the fall in any way. After some years, our institution bought a bus and this actually openedthe world to us. Since we were a a bit grown up, it was the time when some of my seniors and my classmates used to utilize the waiting time in the evening to go and get snacks from a shop that was located in the nearby distance. The feeling of "wonder" was always with me during those times and probably this made my life a very interesting one then. I valued the shop so much because my school mates were buying, and often I too used to go and get some snacks. Out of all the snacks, "chips" was the most famous one. The shop was a small one and the owner was a fat man who used to have a pre-parceled stuff that facilitated his business. The price was mediocre and I remember it to be1 rupee, but still my parents were too careful to put money into my hands. We continued to stay in the same school building till 1985, after which the school got shifted to a different location which was far away from the present location and my home. The long bus travel gave me immense thrill as we used to keep chatting throughout our journey. In a way, it developed new friendship which has become almost a lifelong one. The passage of time drifted the school to a different spot and the new location was a bigger one with lots of buildings. It was built in a modern way and here the beautiful lawn that was semicircle in shape did thrill us a lot. As we entered the school quite early, we used to spend a lot of time loitering in the premises. Often, during winters, we used to plough through the heavy dewdrops that sit on the sleeping grasses of the morning. There were paddy fields all around the school premises and to forget a small theatre in nearby distance would be a great sin. There were times, especially in my 8th standard, when songs were played from the theatre from 11'o clock in the morning. The theatre probably had a speaker outside to attract crowds and therefore every morning, when classes were going on, the music party began with the religious songs. A song that begins with *Vinayagane Vinaitheer pavane*[15] was the one that was played every day. Actually, it gave me a special thrill to listen to the songs, as it made me feel warmth of the home. There was also a nursery near our 8thStd classroom and it was the place that was used by our music teacher to sing songs. We used to sing songs, but often it ended up with laughter, and after some time the music classes faded away from the school due to unknown reasons. Our lunch place was popular for its location as it was far away from our classroom. As each class had its own spot, our spot was at the farthest distance in the football ground near the goal post. We had spent a lot many hours here having lunch and enjoying ourselves in chat. We used to see the cows and sheeps grazing on the comfortable afternoons and there were "touch me not" plants that amused us then. Though classes went on, there were freehours that gave people like me a lot to enjoy. Tirupalai was the placewhere our school was located which was then an undeveloped area that

---

15   A Tamil devotional song

had sparse residential buildings. Time rolled too fast that almost my schooling ended up in the year 1993.

Though school preoccupied me most of the time, I would like to mention about my cousins's school that was located near our Gandhi Nagar home. It was at the corner near Aravind eye hospital and small blocks interposed with dry plain ground. Trees were conspicuous by its absence and yellow buildings were filled with students who were hundreds in number. There was a fence around the school and it was known to people as "Mother Rose" English school. Many a times, I used to accompany my aunt to pick up my brother and sister from this institution. After some years, the school was shifted near JJ hospital in the Golcha complex Road.

In the early days of my boyhood, my haunt was usually around the bus stand, Anna nagar, Sivagangai road and Arvind eye hospital road. I used my 18 inch to explore new places and spots. I used to park my cycle in the shed where there was a car and scooter already in its position. I was very particular that the cycle should not get even a minute scratch and therefore used to negotiate the little space that was available between the car and the scooter to park it in the interior part of the shed. It was a red one and my cousin used to challenge me to share it with her. She used to have an advocate's mind and often used to discuss the legalities of sharing. But stopped cycling after she grew up, and I was free to roam within the above borders. Anna bus stand used to be a busy place then as buses that were plying to Trichy, Thanjavur and other surrounding places were parked there. The road near the bus stand was full of interesting shops of which a bakery by name "V.P.Mathura" was very famous. Its location was exactly behind my Gandhinagar house. When we used to loiter at the backyard during afternoons we have often inhaled the sweet fragrance of cakes in our nostrils. I used to often visit the bakery along with my brother to get veg puffs that was famous then. There were also couple of restaurants nearby and it was always a great feeling for us to visit the hotels along with our parents. One restaurant that was often visited by us as a family was *Arti hotels* near bus stand.

One fact that did not strike us then was fear. There was nothing like hygiene and health consciousness, as we always tasted every available thing without any hesitation. Sugarcane juice was an interesting example and the blue rusted machine was having a big crushing wheel. The man who sold the juice used to labor hard to move the wheels to produce the essence. There used to be big vessels on which the essence got collected and the seller used to filter it and put some ice to serve the customers. Though it sounds unfascinating to read, in reality it was unhygienic as the man never followed any rules. The glasses that were served were not washed appropriately as he used to dip all the glasses in the same big bucket that had water. But despite all these things, we never hesitated to taste the juice at regular times. The bus stand also had a Lala Sweet Shop that was located at the centre of the city bus stop in the bus stand. It was a shop that was painted blue and it was a favorite one for many. "Rajeswari Hotel" was another inseparable part of Gandhi Nagar as it has been there from my very childhood. Till now, the restaurant and lodge remain as it was in the past with the brown paint. Just adjacent to the Lodge, there was a rickshaw stand where atleast five to six rickshaws were parked then. A lot of foot prints lie in this area and memories still hang quite heavily in the minds of the persons who had lived there.

At the right angle to the bus stand, a road cut to Sivaganga, which therefore was termed as the Sivaganga road. This was another famous spot as it was the road where Mini photo studio – a popular one then-was located. There were also a couple of restaurants that served delicious foods. I need to recount a shop that was then known as "Jawahar" hotel serving exceptional parottas. My first experience with Parottas began there and it was so fascinating that even now I would boldly state that I had the best Parottas in that shop. But time's fingers turned the pages leaving the past to the individual minds. A music shop was located just on the left side of the same road. It was in late 1980s and it was a time when music was so popular. Illayaraja was at his peak and people like me tried to trace each and every song that came out of him. Though we had a tape recorder, I personally never attempted to record songs. I had seen Sony, TDKCassettes in my home and therefore felt the urge to visit this shop some day. The day arrived and with the song list in my hands, I pedaled my way to the shop. I remember that it was closed then and I had waited for 40 minutes or so to meet the audio shop owner. I bought an old cassette from my house and gave the list to him asking him to record the songs. He asked me to come two days after and on the allotted day I went with great excitement. I went before the slated time and was shocked to hear from the owner that the cassette was old to record. It was a green Sony cassette and I was made to believe that only standard cassettes should be played in the tape recorder. I never knew for long that such standard cassettes were available in shop itself. But the shop owner boosted my spirits by saying that he had "Meltrack" cassettes and I reluctantly agreed because it was an Indian made one. Still I was excited to play the songs very loud and that was my first experience with the audio recording. Audio recording continued for many years after we shifted out of Gandhi Nagar to P & T Nagar. I learnt about Vijeyam recordings in Goripalayam. This was a small shop and here a dark tall man used to sit with lots cassettes all around him. Buying Cassettes was a great experience for me then, and I had spent a lot of money buying new movie cassettes. I used to give a long list of songs in the shop and got new and old songs recorded in 60 and 90 type ones. But soon, there was a time when the shop was closed for reasons unknown. The musicals did shift to the first floor and there too I visited to finally wash my hands off from music. I don't know the reasons, but my addiction for music and TV had seen its rise and fall.

At the same period there entered something called "Dek"- this was how the Video player was called. It was a time when there were lots of video cassette shops and there was was one opposite to Priya complex christened as *Velankanni*video shop. We used hire the VCD player from this shop and watch five to eight movies in two days. As VCR became popular, almost all homes started purchasing this luxury. But the entry of cable system ruined everything from video shops to theatres. Pyramid Video shop in KK nagar was the biggest one.

****

Goripalayam is Madurai's nerve centre, though people may dispute it in many ways. The century old Albert Bridge with small platforms allowed two-way traffic for long, though experts had warned against overburdening the construction. So, after a particular time, when Shri.P.T.R. PalanivelRajan was the speaker, a new bridge was erected adjacent to the old one and it helped to ease the burden of the former one. The bridge that is being spoken about is above river Vaigai and in a way it connects two different Madurais. *Goripalayam* is on the other side of the bridge that is primarily non-commercial. It is a spot that has a high density of population with lots of houses at close proximity. It is a popular shopping spot that had lots of eateries, cassettes shops, the famous Thevar Statue, Tamukkam grounds and the century old American College. The most popular shop from the early eighties that had attracted a large number of customers is Vijeyams. It is a shop that does not know "nay" in any way. From my childhood days, I have been a frequent visitor of this shop with my father to buy various school based stationeries. A glass jar with red cherries had often tempted me from my boyhood days. It was in the same place for long and not only that, there were also many more chocolates and sweets that had tempted me then. "Fivestar" was the most popular chocolate in 1980s and there was always a craze amongst the boys to go for it. The owner of the shop was a lean dark man whose way of handling the money used to be an exceptional one for boys like me. The way he thrusts the coins forwards to the customer need many eyes to see. This shop had every stationary item in it and even trivial items were found in its shelves. In 1980s and 1990s, there would not have been a person in Madurai to have kept away from Vijeyams. But misfortune fell on the shop in late 1990s as there was a problem amongst share holders that brought down the shutters almost permanently to this two decade old popular shop that was part and parcel of the Madurai life. Two other shops that would be etched in Madurai people's memory was almost near to the above mentioned shop. The first one I wish to mention here is 'Bharath Studio' which was special in every way as it evoked the feeling of 1970s when we entered the shop. It was a shop that was plastered with brown mica, and an entry in to the inner part gave the feeling of being in a blue painted location. This was used by the photographer to click the photos of his customers. Something in the shop disturbed many a person who visited and it was the presence of historical photos. The pictures that were clicked in the early 1970s were very much present in the studio and it often disturbed the serene customers. The next in line is the "Golden Tailors" that was located near the American College. It is an interesting tailor shop that was famous in the late 1970s and early 1980s,after which its popularity waned. As a boy I have also visited the lady's tailor shop atop the golden tailors. One thing that touched me about this shop is the beautiful scent that was hanging throughout the years. The same perfume that I inhaled when I was a boy hung on for a long time almost till the shutters were down. It was a shop that was preferred by my mother and aunts, and whenever we visited the shop, I had the fortune of tasting the chilled flavored milk in theAavin stall that was peeped out from the

American College fore wall. The long platform running from Golden tailors to the King Metro hotel at the other end was an interesting one for people who had the eye to enjoy the beauty of Madurai. City Shop, Narasus Coffee, Ark Bakery, Kumar shirts, SundaramSarees and many more interesting shops were located in the stretch. At times there was a paan shop and once during my boyhood days I was enamored by the paan stuff and ordered for a *Beeda*[16]. I was under the impression that costly *Beeda* has more quality in it, but it took me to a shaky world. The moment it touched my taste buds there emerged a strange sensation with a rapid rotation of everything around me. I spat the stuff and managed somehow to walk to my home unscathed after sitting for minutes in front of the 'Tansi' showroom. 'Tansi' was spot that reminded the last vestiges of the twentieth century. Though it was necessary for people to get into each and every shop, the bustle and the liveliness gave a fresh energy to the people who walked along the stretch of Goripalayam.

Tamukkam Ground is one of the most important parts of Madurai's cultural life, as during summers, there used to be an exhibition that was very popular amongst Madurai people. Though the entry of Multimedia did suck away the vitality of the fair, the importance and popularity of the latter in the bygone days has no words to explain. The advertisements, the voices that speak in the speakers, the transparent bubbles, the archways and the buzz of people give a sort of zest to the exhibition. Long bamboo sticks tied together separated the entry point into different rows which took the visitors to the ticket counter after which people are supposed to enter the ground and through multiple entry points in the archway. A lot of entertainments in various forms were very much there in the ground and simply it was a great sense of wonder for people like me. I am unable to efface the memories pertaining to the giant Pappads and ice creams that were available in the fair. The shops that sold various

---

16   A betel pan used all over India

toys that satisfied the whims of all the young boys was always a centre of attraction for us. The soap water and the round handle through which the young boys blew to produce transparent bubbles are still afresh in my mind. Often, we used to come out of the grounds and take car to reach our residence, but there also were times when we used to walk the two kilometer stretch between the grounds and the residence. The time was such that boys like us never felt tired nor felt the sweat of summer. Since my cousins from Tirunelveli were there, we really had a great time then in this ground. Everytime we visited the fair, the experience was almost similar without much change. But I am pretty sure that for long I never missed the opportunity of visiting the exhibition. Even after getting married, I was a regular visitor to the satiate the urge of my young son. Now, as I sit and muse at those glorious days,I feel the pain of nostalgia aching and squeezing my shapeless mind.

Mind is a strange thing that often oscillates between the past and the present without any charted course. I often struggle to stream line the gush of memories that overflows and leaves me overwhelmed with little consciousness of the present times. In that way, I would like to reminisce the state of some of the important roads in Madurai. Roads are the arteries and veins of a town, through which the life blood pushes its way. Madurai as a town had always been busy and as a child I had never seen an empty Madurai. Even now, flashes of the Diwali time strikes me and I remember a time that was long ago when I ploughed my way along with my father to the tailor shop that was christened as "Raja Tailors". It was a period when readymades were rare, and the fashion was to get the clothing material in metres, and give it for stitching. So, such a system not only made the people go into the tailor shop, but also brought in the exceptional talents of the tailors. Madurai had some exceptional shops which was crowded throughout the year in those days. A shop that was exceptionally popular from 1985 to 1987 was *Paradise tailors* that was located somewhere near the Meenakshi Amman temple. It was the time when 'tight' pant were very famous and they were experts in it. The perfection that was brought in stitching was amazing, but after few years of popularity, they closed the doors for unknown reasons. Some said that they had moved to Gulf, but their perfection is missed by us even now. G.Tex and Super tailors were popular stitchers in 1980s and the latter was so famous amongst the younger lots. Their shop was located in the parallel road adjacent to AV bridge on the way to *Meenakshi College for Women* and there were times when we had to wait for a long time till measurement was taken. The owner was one Anandhan, a Malayali, who was quite smart and was a very diplomatic and intelligent person. In the due course, he shifted his shop to a new location at the junction of Thevar statue. Since he was a family friend of us, our whole family stitched our dresses there that included uniforms, wedding suites, festival dresses and many more dresses for many more important occasions. Even now, the shop has the same old guy as employee and most of them are said to be his relatives. The road that was parallel to AV bridge had two wings, the left and the right wing.

A person who comes from Goripalayam can take either the left parallel road or the right parallel road with both leading to the Vaigai river. The roads were dusty on the leftside with lots of timber shops and crossing the same, we come across the river, after which, the road turns to right and crosses the bridge in the subway manner. The river was mostly dry with dirty waters trickling with weeds overgrown in every nook and corner. There were dhobis performing their task with gusto and white clothes were left on the plain ground for drying. The rotten smell that enters your nostrils brings thoughts that are repellent and dirty. But things were not same, for rainy season brought copious water and in 1980s there were many instances of the waters submerging the *chinnapalam*[17], a bridge that was parallel

---

17   A small bridge that is adjacent to AV bridge

to AV bridge. It was just a connective road that brought peoples from Yanaikal and deposited them in Sellur. When it came to rains, the great rains of 1993 need mention as there was a continuous downpour for more than five days.

It was literally a non-stop rain and our family was glued to our house in Pasupathinagar. Morning and evenings brought no change and after a couple of days there was even a power cut that left us in a lurch. The glaring wet roads with sticky leaves and furrowed mud are still are damp in our minds. After few days of heavy rains, I visited KK Nagar 80 ft road and met a classmate of mine who was so excited and was literally playing in a pool of water. It was Diwali eve and when I told of my plans to visit Thanjavur, he bluntly said it is not possible as the roads are broken and the connection is cut in many routes. I would boldly assert that Madurai never saw such heavy rains after 1993, the so called "Global Warming" had changed the whole order. It was the time when I saw our late Chief Minister J. Jayalalitha,ploughing through the broken roads along with her huge convoy.

Race course is the *Lords of Madurai* and the road that edged through it was deserted and well maintained. From the days when I started to travel through the school bus, it had a special attraction for me as it connected the District court and Pudur. The road that used to wind its way through the peripheries of the play ground on the left and the electricity board office on the right was used by the driving school people for teaching their wards the art of driving cars. A hostel that was on the left side of the road and it is still the same. It is not the breadth of the road that attracted me, but the actual silence and deserted look had touched me. Our bus driver who used to plough through the traffic snarls, suddenly raised the speed limit in the race course road. The big open ground on the left side had hosted special football and cricket matches on different occasion.. When we were school boys and when I was staying in Annanagar, I usually visit the ground every morning to play Cricket. It was half yearly holidays and I and my cousin (who had come for holidays) used to pedal our way to the ground to play the game of Cricket. It was in 1989 and it was the time when the illustrious Sachin Tendulkar made his debut against Pakistan. The period was such that there was no crowd in the ground as it is now. The consciousness of physical exercises and walking was not there and it left the place empty. The road did not have any shop, but used to have strange men who used to come and sit along with their friends for unknown reasons. The road ends in a junction which on the right side would take the passengers to Pudur, while the straight road would take a venture in to the DRO Colony and left one would lead to Pandiyan hotels. Thus the road mentioned above was an impressive one despite its general unimportance in term of significance.

Just opposite to the American College there was a small road that had some interesting shops. It was again an insignificant road that led to the inner parts of Goripalayam. In 1990s as college students, the young ones used to spend their time in the chat shop on the left side of the road. The shop was christened as 'Chit-Chat' and it was very famous amongst the college students. It was a small shop with barely three or four tables and stools. Literally, it was a fashion for the American College students to step into their shop to have a fag and tea. They also provided 'Samosa' with sauce which was equally popular. I know not for what reasons I visited this shop; but many a time I had tasted the tea and 'samosa' and at times have also smoked as it was an age that made us feel stronger with cigar in our fingers. The owner was a SriLankan Tamil and he was an active guy who bonded with many people. Next to the shop, there was a two wheeler mechanic shop that had two person of which one was a small guy. The third shop in the same row was *Sami Kadai*[18].

SAMI- OWNER IN HIS POPULAR TEA SHOP

The owner was an oldman for long and was quite popular amongst the student community and the shop was a small one with no much space for chairs nor stools, but it had a long bench on the corner. The

---

18   A shop that was near The American College frequented by the students

customers here too were College Students and mostly they smoked and loved to sit on the steps that were nearby. Here tea is used to be served in the glass tumbler in contrast to the stainless steel servings in chit-chat. It may all sound silly, but it were great times that still steams with heat. The small road was not only busy, but also was notorious for murders once. But despite all these things, the Xerox shop was full with people. Those are great days and it would have been fine then, to have measured the number of visits we made to shops in and around. Here, I should not miss the sweet shop that was directly opposite to the American College and it was the *Alankar*[19] Sweets. It was a traditional shop that was modern in outlook and one interesting fact is that it had been in the same place for more than two decades. The tea that was served here was special with lots of spices added to it and here too *Samosa* was famous. The shop had a comfortable space for sitting and usually the PG guys relaxed here as they often loved to have tea with their girl friends at this spot. The owner was a tall guy with curly hair and he was always neatly dressed with tucked in shirt. He literally maintained the solemnity of the shop in all possible ways. There was an empty deserted place near the shop with rusted iron gates and overgrown weeds. It had made me wonder about the owner of the place and why it had been locked

In the Goripalayam main road, there was a bus stop and it was an attractive junction as it was crowded all the time. For many years, the bus stop is at the same location with lots of Tea shops. Malliga coffee bar is located at the bus stop along with a sweet stall nearby. There is also a khadi shop, a tailor shop and the most popular tiffin centre known as MudaliyarIdliKadai, NMP Bakery, Samad tailors etc. The platform is the place where all the commuters are supposed to stand, but here most of the peoples stand in the road. The buses that stop at this Junction usually try to keep away from the busy road by almost Jamming the vehicle near the platform. The broken platform blocks

---

19   A sweet shop cum mini restaurant opposite to The American College

that were uneven in certain spots has the potential to push a person down, but Madurai people are quite skilled in managing the issue. It is difficult thing for a person to board the bus in afternoons generally; the buses are sparse though the crowd was heavy. I remember the days when as school boy doing his 10thstd, sweating it out in the bus while moving towards my destination. Of the lot of surprises I have come across, the tree that is found in the Goripalayam bus stop had been there for many decades without getting disturbed. It shaded the commuters who were waiting for the bus. Though a mystery, it is fully used by the people for advertisement purposes. As one can see few steel plates pasted or nailed on the tree. The poor tree also bears a long rope hanging from a decent height with one end tied to the tree, while the tip has embers live enough to light a cigar. Yes, people in Madurai are highly innovative and even a rope is used by them for business purposes. Those were times when I was not so health conscious and therefore loved to taste the fruit juices prepared in these shops without hesitation. But only after my PG did I realize that some of the shops there were using waters from the nearby public toilets and from then on kept away even from tasting tea. It would be an interesting walk from the bus stop to the post office that was located on the far end of the road that was popularly called as Alagarkovil road. A pedestrian can come across a couple of old tailor shops, and in our graduation days, there was a famous gift shop that sold greeting cards. Since, the American college was nearby, the business went on in full swing as it was in pre-mobile times. Young people would love to gift their friends and lovers with cards and I remember the "Valentine days" time when the shop was almost full. Literally I came to hear about Valentine's Day only after I became an UG student in the American college. People especially, the younger lots made a big buzz out of the day. So this spot had a special place in our memories as it was the last remnant of the pre-mobile communications. The people knocked the door of this shop for every festival that included 'Diwali', 'Christmas','Newyear' and 'Pongal'. The cards were great conveyors of love and affection throughout India. Courier services were less in numbers,and it was viewed with suspicion by people as they relied more on the post offices to send the greeting cards. As a result, the post office that was located just opposite to *Tamukkam*[20] grounds was very busy during the day time,and less busy during night times.

TAMUKKAM GROUNDS DURING SUMMER FAIRS

It was located in the right-hand corner of the four road junction near the traffic beat. The office was big enough to accommodate both people and vehicles. The post van that used to be red in colour often enters and exits the cemented outer floors of the office. There used to be variety of post boxes near the parking lot with each box signifying

---

20   A vast expanse of land used for political and public meetings. located at the heart of Madurai

a destination. Local letters could be dropped into the local boxes that were green in colour with the mention of the collection time in it. Likewise, different destination had different box and there was a table inside the office with a lot of sticky glue in it. It was for the customers who would purchase covers and stamp to paste and post it. The office was very busy and often I saw three wings of people, with the first wing sitting in the entrance to sell stamps, collect speed post letters, weigh the letters and parcels. The second wing had senior people who sat and they were busy with other worksand there were superior officers who could be reached only with permission and special purposes. Thus 1980s and 1990s treated the post offices with remarkable respect, and now things have turned topsy-turvy with offices losing its charm and their business to the courier services. Though people say that Indian life could be divided by the year 1991 into two, I would say that year 2002 is significant as it was the time when mobile phones became famous and initiated the modernity that left the past order to crumble. Presently it is sad to even cross the post office as it appears to be relic of the past with deserted look. But it is not only empty due to the socio economic changes that had taken place in the past twenty years, but is at the verge of closure in few years from now.

There are other spots in Madurai that are tantalizingly beautiful and conventional in nature. Alagarkovil is one such spot that has a large baggage of traditionalism in it. The beautiful temple with massive space and disturbing monkeys can never be erased from one's memory. It is almost unchanged and even now when I visit the temple, I find similarity to the 1980s and 1990s as time has been slow to change the atmosphere. A good deal of trekking is possible in the mountain that is a part of the temple location. In 1997, we as students of the The American college did visit the spot and spent a lot of hours under the trees in this holy mount. A walk through the mountain will lead you to a hill temple called *Palamudhircholai*

Where Lord Muruga graces the devotees. The lush green shrubs and trees that form a part of the mountain give a scenic experience of the onlookers who visit the spot regularly. Since the temple is a bit faraway from the city, it is not possible for all to visit the holy premises regularly. It is common for people to visit it as a tourist spot than a holy spot.

On the way to Alagarkoil lies the infamous Pudur which is often known as K.Pudur. It is one of busiest area in Madurai and also a popular residential area. It has a shapeless bus stand surrounded by a lot of shops that sell a variety of things right from greens to cloth. As young boy, I had visited Pudur in a town bus along with my aunt and the purpose was to visit the construction site of my uncle's home. The fish market was very popular then, and even now I remember the smell of the fish market in that locality. It has many narrow streets which often crisscrossed with various roads to finally connect with the new Natham and old Natham road. In 1990s, when I had shifted to Pasupathinagar, I often take this route in scooter to reach Pudur. I had often wondered at the small roads with ditches and houses on both the sides taking one through a very illustrious, uncomfortable ride. The problem with the Pudur main road is that there were lots of vendors on the roadside, selling a whole lot of things from flowers to groundnuts.

The busy Pudur is same as it was thirty years ago with few changes here and there, though the population has multiplied in a manifold manner. Like Pudur, there was another busy place which is known more as a residential location than a pure shopping spot. K.K. Nagar was a posh area in 1980s and the 80 feet road that houses "The Hindu" office and Remuki showroom was a much sought after one in those days. When I was in Annanagar, one of my friend took me to a shop in K.K.Nagar and it was a time when we pedaled all the way from Annanagar to this shop. It was a snack shop which was known then as "Sangam sweets". It was a popular location where most of the couples from the nearby institutions parked themselves to have amusing time. It was the first time, I tasted the so called "Paanipuri" and honestly speaking I was bit shy to go the shop as I often felt that it was open only for seniors. But that experience stood for a long time and even after many years, I visited the shop to satiate my taste buds. This friend of mine by name Manish was a North Indian and had a great contact with many local shops and I was introduced to many eateries by him. "Ramesh bakery" is another location in the road that connected the Suguna stores and Aravind eye hospital. It was another shop introduced by the same guy and here we used to have tasty puffs. This was the time when I stayed in AnnaNagar, a place that was silent and decent. It was a small house and I remember me and the guy visiting a tuition centre in Mahatma Montessori School. Mahatma school was located in Annanagar and it was not a very rich location. The institution then, was handling tuition classes for other school students every evening after the school time. A middle aged dark guy by name Rangarajan was our teacher and he taught us mathematics. It is unknown if we benefitted through the tuitions, but the location and the experiences we had there are striking. It was in Annanagar when I was a school student, did the inauguration of Ambiga theatre happen. I think it was in the year 1989 and it was a time movies and theatres were very famous amongst the people. A lot of cine stars had descended into Madurai that day and I was very happy to know about the theatre inauguration which was quite near my home. I remember many things in Anna Nagar as I was a steady roamer with a thorough knowledge about the vein and arteries of Anna Nagar. Never would I forget the days when I used to play cricket in front of Manish's home. It was a narrow street and we drew the stumps in the wall and allowed the batsman to hit only on the offside. Luckily there were no ditches and there was no need for us to wash the ball. Days went by and in few years time we shifted to P&T Nagar that was totally different from the life I lead in Gandhi Nagar and Anna Nagar. For the first time I came across an 'U' shaped deviation the bus took from the main road and the locality was a residential one known as Viswanathapuram. Here one can come across an old yellow coloured theatre that was known as Vijayalakshmi. It was a 'B' grade theatre that slowly faded away with time. The only problem from the point is that the road becomes considerably narrow and it takes a long stretching lane until the terminus is reached. The nerve centre of P&T nagar is Valluvar Colony that was predominantly occupied by the Saurashtra community. They were weavers by profession and even in the early 1990s, one could come across yarns spread in the mud lane of Valluvar colony. A small Shiva temple with grills and gates occupied the left hand corner on the main road load. If at all, I have come across a dull locality in my life, it is none but this. There was also a shop on the right side of the main road and it was peculiar for me then as there was a fat guy running the canteen. It was a multifaceted shop as it had an eatery, a cooking spot, a house as well as a video shop. Everything belonged to the same family and hygiene was rich in its absence as the shop was dirty, but the video shop as it is was evenmore conspicuous by its filth.

    The terminus or end of P&T nagar road was such that the buses were generally parked at an empty plot that was nearby my home. By constantly looking at the buses, I developed a sort of affinity for it that I could guess the number of the bus through its engine sound, horn and the timing. '48P' was my favorite bus and I know not for what reason it was my favorite. It was silver colored one with 'orangish' yellow mica looking alike, but longer than the other buses. It was neither new nor old then. The horn of this bus was an attraction and I loved to travel in it. I was quite thorough with timings and its first entry was at 7.20, and the next one was at 10.30 and the last trip was at 9.30pm and everytime I heard the bus sound I used to come out to look into it. It was the time when suddenly the drivers and conductors changed the colour of their uniforms and I wondered for long, before I understood that the blue uniforms signified the experience ladder they were in. Just opposite to my house there was an empty compounded plot where one bold lady called Mariyamma resided. She used to do household duties and also performed various errands to the people who were nearby. She was also laden with all the local news that we stopped listening to Radio for some time. There was a temple at some distance and it was at its beginning with only "*Vinayagar*" at the centre, while the other spots remaining empty.

More than the above mentioned temple, there was one that was more popular in terms of devotee numbers and power. It was a very small temple that was located in the main road not far from the middle of it. It was called as "Karupanaswamy Temple" which was just a small rectangular one with conically protruding structure followed by Hundial at the right side it. A lot of lances were pierced in the ground and many bells did hang behind the structure. It was a deity that presided over the locality like Pattimedu. In those times, Pattimedu was considered to be a dangerous locality and in 1990s the roads were more or less deserted. There were fields on the both sides of the road and water channel used to be full, providing irrigation to the cultivation. In the early 1990s when there were scarcely any residential buildings nearby, I used to stand in terrace to watch the massive mountain that was afar and at times have spotted flames shining on these rocks. It used be nice to stand on the flat terrace with full moon glowing at its maximum strength and silence enveloping the whole spot, except for the insects that moan around the street lamps. It was a practice for us to sit on the terrace in the steel chairs and chat for a long time. The 1990s was not so different from the previous decade as there were no massive changes. The streets were lit with tube lights and cars were almost scarce, for only taxis and ambassadors were famous then. In my school days, I had the habit of riding in my bicycle to school premises and I usually took the

Meenakshinagar route. It was a road that cut left from the main road and passed through the old buildings of P&T nagar roads. P&T nagar roads were uneven and often ended in a mud road junction that had a small bridge over the water channel. I had often come across people taking bath here, and there were also ones who washed clothes, but in those times I never thought nor admired the beauty of the spot though I remember the red sand road that took one to *Paloorani*[21] village that had thatched houses in clusters. Big trees were shading the roadside and I had never been comfortable in this road. So, from P&T nagar, I rode straight to the Meenakshi nagar area which took 'S'type diversion to make me join the main road which was called Narayanapuram junction. From there I had to ride few kilometers to reach *Tirupalai*[22]. In 1990s the traffic was very less, while the roads were big enough to invite people to use them. The big pond on the left side of *Narayanapuram* had water throughout the year and had a temple nearby that is even now famous amongst the folks. I would like to recount few incidents of my college days as the next decade was mostly spent in college. I joined The American College in the year 1993 and it was a practice then to wait for the bus at P&T nagarbus stop. Though initially I waited alone to catch the bus, soon, I got a lot of unreliable guys as companions. We used to wait just opposite to the Karupannaswamy temple near the compound wall of a house. It was a grey unplastered wall that was used for laying the books as it was deemed abnormal for a college student to have a bag with them. Often, I had a couple books with me and used to wait there. The age was such that we were often slipping into vortex of love and just afar from us, near some thorny weeds, there used to wait a bevy of girls for the buses. Bold I was then that I picked up conversations with them with my broken English. I knew not the knack of acquainting with girls that I had often turned out to be

---

21   A hamlet near p&tnagar
22   A far away location where the JV school was located

a villain, while real villains paired well. There were also guys who played pranks by creating false notions of love which people like me literally believed. But years passed and every time we got into the bus, mostly No-11, there used to be a huge crowd and honestly we loved standing. At time we also stood on the footboard and some time I was also down in every stop allowing people to enter and exit through the doorway. I don't know for what reasons I took such risks, but to think of those experiences gives me goose bumps. There were two girls who fascinated me in those days of which the first one was a PG student who was studying in the Meenakshicollege, while the second one was a literature student in Lady Doak College. Lady Doak College had always thrilled the American college students and even the most ordinary girl was admired by us if she was from that college. The girl whom I mentioned above was from Kerala and I fell in love with her just for the reason that her fingers brushed with my shirt one evening unintentionally in the bus. Though it did not create any sensation in me, a guy by name Arun coaxed me by making me believe that she was in love with me. Like a lovelorn youngster, I kept the flame alive for few weeks and eventually handed over a proposal card on the Valentine's day. I was so immature during those times that I was stalking her for some time, till her brother whom people said, was a big rowdy from Pune landed in Madurai. My friends were so good that they forcibly made me meet him. It was a strange meeting and I was very much embarrassed, though the people around me were expecting great scenes. Luckily, all is well that ends well and the 'Pune rowdy' left the scene without much fuss. The other girl I was following up was a sweet curly haired one with a fresh flowery face, a 'sonnet' like smile. She always came in sarees and she was so so beautiful that I usually waited for her on my return trip to come in 3B/11 bus though she was seated far away from me. She never spoke a single word with anyone, but I understood a lot from her eyes. Time has dried my love petals, but the fragrance is ever fresh.

Madurai did not have any interesting parks and the only entertainment for most of the people is theatre. It is theatre and nothing else, and luckily Madurai had many interesting theatres throughout. The most frequented theatre then was Priya complex that had three screens *Cine priya, Mini priya, Sugapriya*[23] of which the first one was a big one that did not have any air-conditioner then. It was quite old with cinema scope screen or 70mm screen as it was called then. *Sugapriya* was the most popular one as it was an air-conditioned one with decorative lights and cushion seats. In 1980s, I visited this complex very often and the movies that were released here were mostly super hits. Two movies did impress me a lot, of which *Agni Natchatirum* was the first one and *Idhayathai Thirudathe* was the second one. We, as a family visited the theatre during summer noon through the side gates and there used to be massive crowds. Many a times we did not get tickets, but for movies like *Agni Natchatiram*, we got through counter. It was an enjoyable experience and buying the ticket and watching for the movie is the most thrilling experience a person can ever have. The rich ice cream and hot popcorn were an enjoyable treat for the movie goers like me. "IdhayathiThirudathe" movie was initially a dumb one, but had a late pick up and being a student of 9th std on the verge of adolescence, it in fact, created a sensation. Sadly I tried hard to watch this movie as I did not get any chance to do so. In those days, at least till 9th std; we were not allowed to visit the theatres alone. I got the chance only when one of my uncle's was in Madurai and through him I enjoyed the movie. It was virtual celebration in those days and in summer times, almost every movie were a hit. It is not only Priya complex, there was also a theatre nearby my home in Gandhi nagar in 1980s and it was the famous *Sha* theatre. It was facing the riverbed and in childhood times, hit movies like *Vidhi, Erandilondru, Jeeva, Giraftaar*[24] and such

---

23   A popular theatre complex in Anna nagar
24   Movie titles

other movies were screened there. It was a big theatre without any Air-conditioner. If the family decides to go for a movie, we used to rush an hour earlier to buy tickets and watch the movie.

There was one theatre near Periyar bus stand which was known then as *Thanga Regal*[25]. It was a peculiar theatre as it had much other entertainment apart from movies. Especially, there was a club called Victorian club and a whole lot of people were members and evenings were spent by those people in a joyous way. I used to visit this theatre with my father and once when I was in theatre, I had a special thrill of getting a chance to collect 'Gold Spot' topper cap sometime early in 1980s. My school was abuzz with a rubber cartoon picture round in shape and it was told by my friends that it comes in gold spot cap. The *Gold spot* was a bottled drink that was tasty in its own way. It had an orange flavor and colored with special attraction for younger ones. In order to boost up the production and sales they had come up with a special rubber picture that was placed behind a cap for collection, one could take the rubber picture and store it as a precious collection and we loved to collect and it made us love Gold spot. There were many other drinks in 1980s, like *Torina, Maaza and Parner*[26] that were popular in their own way. It was in the *Regal* theatre, did I get a chance to collect the gold spot cover and I continued the collecting hobby for sometime before it all stopped. Theatres like *Nadana, Natiya, Thangam, Sundaram*[27] and in fact far away theatres like *Madhu, Amirdham* were all attraction spots for common folks like us. Of all these theatres, it was *MapillaiVinayagar* in the by-pass road that was special to me. Not that the English movies were released here, but the atmosphere of the theatre was such that every individual would love to spend time here. One movie that had a terrific impact on me during the latter half of 1990s was "Titanic", it gave an immense

---

25 A popular theatre near busstand
26 Indian soft drinks in pre liberallised era
27 Theatres

thrill to watch the movie. The last movie I watched in this theatre was also in late 1990s and the movie was "Beach". Though it was big dragging one, it was a special one at the age. Madurai theatres were wide spread and it could be spotted in every part of Madurai. Right from posh locality to a slum like spot, theatres were everywhere. But now after more two and half decades, it is painful to see most of the theatres getting closed and some are in a dilapidated condition. Times change everything and it is shocking to see the great change that had taken place in Madurai.

Meenakshi Amman Temple is the identity of Madurai and I have been fortunate to visit the temple right from my childhood in different circumstances. My devotion and love for the temple has changed with age and circumstance, for in my childhood days, I remember going to temples in the car with the whole family members packed into it. Most of the Fridays, our family would knock the door of GoddessMeenakshi. We used to ferry into the busy Simmakkal area and pass through a sandal wood shop which was a source of attraction for us then, as there were two beautiful dolls on the shop.

Fortunately even after forty years when I pass through the street, I find the same shop with same dolls doing their business. The vendors and the small shops on the narrow road were always busy, the only difference is that cars were scarce then and the most of the traffic snarls were caused by the cycles, rickshaws and the tricycles. The sweet smell of incense and fruits were soothing then, and I was happy with the temple visit on those days as it was followed by a weekend holiday. The car parking was easy, as we used to park the car on the surrounding area of the temple, and the entry was usually through the gate where a small *Vinayagar* was located on the right side of the entry. It was a beautiful *Vinayagar*, and the people used to apply the ashes on the idol and pray. The big pond was full of water then, the big stone wall was an aesthetic one. We went straight into the sanctum sanctorum of Goddess Meenakshi, prayed, and, went to Swami Sannidhi. The perambulations near the Swami Sannidhi was a thrilling one as it had a dark narrow path which me and my brother walked through with thrill. But mostly, interesting segment of our temple visit was the hard *Murukku* and *Appam*[28] we had from the *prasadam*[29] stall that was inside the temple. The shiny floors, high roof, the smell of ash and flowers, the presence of large number of north Indians, bats, the mercury light and the old roof were all great in experience and feeling. I have often felt the temple visit a reassuring one, cleansing all the negativism from the inner recesses of mind. Likewise, the shopping centre around the temple was a joy for the patient beings. There were many famous textiles shops all around, of which *Hajeemoosa* was the most popular one. *Selections*, *Designs* were other shops that were popular in the vicinity. Pudhu Mandapam was a locality that housed all the school bookshops. Madurai was famous for some renowned eateries of which, *Arya*

---

28   A type of snack available in temple stalls
29   An offering given to God

Bhavan[30] had a great popularity amongst the masses along with *The Modern Restaurant*. Everything was tasty and its popularity was such that most of the travelers never missed the chance of checking into these eateries.

Madurai then was a little bit backward and it was the practice for the local vendors to sell their products by moving out in streets. There were many sweet sounds that could be heard in evenings while idling inside the house. The small grey-box like vehicle being peddled by men was a special thrill for us, asbakeries then sold their wares through these tricycles. Often between 5.30pm to 7.30pm, we could hear these men pedaling slowly on the sun burnt streets with a small lamp inside the box. Usually, we used to buy the so called Veg-puffs or coconut buns as it was more popular amongst us. Since it was a joint family, none of us even thought buying and having snacks for ourselves. One other evening vendor was the *Bombay Mittai* push cart that had a closed glass jar into which the sweet (Son Pappadi) used to be stored and customers could pay the money to get the sweet in the news paper pack. There was another jar in the pushcart which had some strange sweets in it, I had often tried those sweets, butwas often left indecisive with the taste. The vendor's voice was a lament, but still appealed to the younger ears. If the weekday evenings saw these vendors, on Saturdays and Sundays we were regular buyers of ice-creams from other vendors. They used to visit during mornings and *Kani ice*-creams were the most popular stuff amongst us. We preferred the mango or grape flavor sticks and we used to drop the ice in a tumbler licking it now and then as slowly as possible. More than the lick, we actually loved to drink the melted essence. There were many other sellers, of which the *State ice* used to offer a cone shaped fruit sticks. Summer vacation made us spend a lot for the ice-creams as anything cool was attractive, and in early 1980s refrigerators were not that popular. *Allwyn* refrigerators came

---

30   A popular Hotel in 1980s and 1990s

into our home in 1984, but failed to work for technical reasons. We waited for few more days to finally taste the chilled waters. Sundays often gave us the *Rasna* drink to beat the heat. The powder and the essence found in the *Rasna* pack gave us the soar taste, but still for the sake of ice cubes we drank the juice with great passion,and time has moved so fast that there is no remnant of any of this popular stuff today. Experiences are tasteless in the present times, but like wine gains value in the future.

After leaving the school, I was so excited as it was a tough time for me then in the school due to an overburdening academic weight. I was so happy to be let off from the academic prison that had taken a toll on my mental health. The agony of being scolded before others was a literal thorn in my mind, and I bled due to my sensitivity. My confidence was eroded and an unknown type of fear engulfed me. The succor to this pain came in the form of the *The American College*. Though my grandfather was eager to put me up in a dental college, I was not up to the mark that eventually settled me in a dull room in the college, but without much interest. But since I did not have any other go, I sat in the first year class room along with fifty other students. Being an institution located in the heart of Madurai, it was the first choice of the student community. The entrance had a Majestic look with grilled transparent forewall that showed few trees and cycle stands. The black stone with whitewordings pronounced the name of the college at the entrance. The reddish orange sand that was not too soft smiled at us in the entrance.

It was strange for me, as it was a new world altogether, and on the very first day I was denied entry into the main hall due to my weak punctuality. The red bricks with century old wrinkles, the hard stones that formed the floor and steps, the prison like gates in the hall, the grey windows, and the high ceiling with wooden support are all the impressions that hang in my mind from that great day.

The problem with the American college is that a sensitive entrant has to manage the overwhelming waves of past that flows past us. It makes us stagnant, wet and something deep in us gets disturbed. The tall trees shading every nook and corner of the expanse is the richest library a person can ever come across. Any student who treads into the campus has to bear the weight of the falling leaves at least for few seconds. Built in a typical western style, the main building is a monument with human presence.

But though I missed the entry into hall, I approached the volunteers who were seated near the gates who asked me to wait behind them till the session was over in the main hall. The students streamed in, and by asking here and there, I entered the classroom to sit in a peculiar American college chair. It was a wooden one with a folding broad hand rest on the right side of the chair, there was also enough space to place our bags at the base of the chair. It was a congested room without any *social distance* as fifty five students sat near each other. The windows were old and creaking without any grill. There were atleast six windows showing up the college and the unknown strange part of the used compound wall that were tall enough for a building. The building that housed us was known as *Flint house* and before I elaborate about it, let me tell something about my first experiences in an English literature class. There was a dais with a black old board lit by a long tube light. The fans were old, but still gave us the needed air. Since everything was shady all around, it was impossible to sit in the classroom without the lights 'On'. But I was sitting idly without much interest as there was always a sense of lethargy in me. The first professor who handled our class was Prof. RajendraPandian who was shortly called as RP. He gave an inspiring speech about English and life in American college, and the way in which he narrated the beauty of the flint house especially during rainy days was impressive.

Days started rolling fast and it was a great time for me as there were few tests and quizzes, with the working hours far lesser than what I had in school. The freedom to bunk the classes made one even more excited and whenever I got absented in the afternoons, I had to forego the classes of Prof. John Sahayam and Prof.Savio, who were great in their own ways. Lunch time was pretty interesting as most of the time I visited my home for good, while on occasions, I did join my classmates to go to the nearby restaurant Ashok Bhavan. It was an old hotel, and I do remember it even during my boyhood days, but the time when we were studying, it was pretty nice to get into the Air-conditioned hall that was inside the restaurant. It had a dull light that was normal in terms of aestheticism, and hardly just eight tables were there. To be honest, the Ac room was mostly unoccupied in those days and I loved to watch the way in which some of my classmates devoured the food. They order for special meals and tire the waiter through their intestinal urge. In the college too, there was a canteen which was antique in appearance. An old man with white moustaches, shaky hands was in charge of it and at times I do step in to have the so called *parottas*. It was located near the ground, far away from the department. Though it was unhygienic in nature, canteen people were so kind that many students used to cheat them without paying the bill. I did not have any special feeling then, but now when I do think of them, I feel ashamed for having been a silent spectator. The stone benches in front of the canteen was always a special one as the shady trees provided refuge for the students from scorching heat and lectures. It was a spot that brought both teachers and students together, and I am literally proud to remember that on many occasions I had a chance to Speak and share tea with my favourite*Prof. DSL*[31].

The cycle stand in the college slowly became the spot for students gathering and friends from the same school but different courses in the college used the stand to meet with one another. It was a time when bikes were slowly replacing the cycles, though the domination of bicycles was a little bit less than in previous times. A lot of my friends eagerly bought Yamaha and Suzuki bikes, while few more were flying in the thin Scooty. But more than all these get togethers, we came to know that the college condoled the death of its retired and working staff. Though initially I did not understand, at a point of the time I understood that these condolence meetings made the students happy as the college was closed for the day if someone died. In this way, we got a lot of holidays and we even prayed on the days of tests and quizzes for the meetings.

There was an old auditorium which still bears the past with it in the form of windows and doors. The grey windows and the unique style of the grills reminded the onlooker about the 1950s and 1960s when probably the building came about. All the departmental programmes

---

31   Former HoD of the English Dept in The American College

and even some plays were staged in this hall. There was a sense of darkness in the hall and during examination times it served as an examination hall as well. *Pegasus*[32], the English department function used to be held in the auditorium and all the guy including few staff member will be highly charged up to show their mettle to the visiting girls. But mostly the love ions were diffused by the invasive sounds that disallowed the boys from getting close to the girls. The irony is that most of us used to dress in a perfect manner on the particular day with a firm faith that we could attract atleast one or two persons. But all the three years ended up in a miserable failure. There was a small store near the auditorium and it is the shop that supplied some of the books that connected us with literature. The American college in Madurai is a town in itself and is self sufficient in all ways, from water to power, everything is available in the campus, and a lot Sprawling bungalows punctuate the green shaded campus. My UG days was a bit raw as it was a bit superficial in nature, and I did not delve deep into the college to know about its nitty-gritties. But even in those days, I had seen a couple of Americans from Shansi University roaming in their two wheelers, but I was least interested in knowing about them. When I entered my PG, the college appeared in a different perspective, as a new world opened unto me. Unlike the swarming *Flint house*, the PG department was at a corner that overlooked the Government Rajaji hospital to its side. The building was known as the *Centenary building*, that had two storeys in it. English department (PG) was in the first storey and it was bridged with the SCILET that was located close to the department library. My first day in the PG department was a bit awkward as I reached the college a bit early in the morning and unlike the UG orientation attended the programme in the main hall, later, we were shown into the department that had a flexible brown door with a peeping glass in between. The floors were of course a bit old with the mosaic holding on to the stains of the past

---

32   A departmental function in The American College

decades. Every wall was white though the usual scratches and dirt was quite prominent throughout. A long dirty parapet wall provided us the view of another building nearby, and it was the department of Botany, and the intervening space was occupied by a decent amount of trees that were certainly old enough to sing the past to the keen ears. There were five rooms altogether in the department with the first room, allotted for the second years, while the next one was for the first years that was followed by a Staff room and the Professor's chamber. The last room was for the students, and those days it was known as the *Lounge*. Easy chairs, massive round table with the chairs all around, studentcupboards and magazine boxes were some of the props that coloured the room. Though initially, as first year guys, we were reluctant even to enter in to the lounge, then we were made to realize the importance of the room. The class rooms were too comfortable with 'U' shaped table arrangements and 'S' type wooden chairs allowing just 15 members into it. The beautiful library though not a great reader myself- was not only impressive but created a sense of burden to the viewers. Lots of books kept staring at us and three rows of tables and chairs smiled at us. The smells of the books were unique and everytime we opened a cupboard to search for some text, a pinching smell of the past pierced through our prowling personality. I had the habit of looking at the borrowers list, the dates especially and would savour at the dates that were printed at the last paper of the book. Often, when I came across the years that were too old, it gave me a thrill that is inexpressible -especially years that denoted 1982, 1983, 1985 – and was making me feel the pulse of the past. I often loved to listen about my seniors from some of the library staff members, who were former PG students. When I came to know about the voracious reading habits of those students, I often got charged up though practicing the same was a bit difficult. I was a great fan of one of my seniors Shri.B.Anand, I.A.S. Though I had met him only once, he inspired me so much that I used to learn a lot of details about him from the Librarian. Literally, PG department was a dream that played on us for long, infact till now its fragments float on us as a broken rainbow unable tosink nor dissolve. But still, the massive SCILET library with its new wooden cupboards and offices offered me a special attraction then.

As the academic machine was at its full steam, one fine day, we were taken by our seniors to a bungalow christened *Boton*[33]. It was the residence of the erstwhile SCILET director, an American by birth, Dr. Paul Love. Though it was a strange experience, it gave me immense pleasure as I had never seen such a beautiful old building that was certainly colonial in outlook. The golden lightings, the complete mat, the library, the twisted colonial wooden steps, the neat bedrooms with white sheets, the balcony and above all the neatness and the wooden smell was refreshing and touching. One unique thing I noticed thenwas the creaking sounds of the fans in all the rooms. Though initially I doubted if someone would be there, later realised through my seniors that all the rooms were open to all, and in the earlier decade students would visit the bungalow as per their wish. It was the first of the series of visits we were to make in the subsequent years, and in fact we tried to get close with the great professor who was the architect of the PG English department. The dinners he gave were extraordinary with the cook Rajan showing his mettle. The beautiful hall with a whole lot of books all around lit with the dull golden lights, we all sat cuddled with one another to listen to the conversations and the songs sung by the inmates. Prof.R.P.Nair, another genius was always there and it was memorable nights.

The green trees and herbiage is something that needs to be wondered in the America college campus and when rains pour in, the dropping sounds are music in itself. In 1993, there was such a heavy rain that every time we were in the examinations hall for

---

33   Asprawling colonial type bungalow in The American College campus

the (November) semester examinations, there used to be a heavy downpour outside. The wet bark of the trees that carries the time's wrinkles often looked sullen for some unknown reasons. Whenever, the college bells tolled the trees shivered to drop more water on the ground. Here, a mention of the bell would be appropriate and it was no doubt a bit unique for the first timers who heard the bell. The bell is located near the canteen on a spot where the dried leaves were resting without any movement, a small red painted shelter was around the bell and a rope hung from its tongue, but was kept virtually at a higher plane that would discourage the students from touching it. The first time I heard it was from my class room that was far away from the department of time. Though I wondered how the sound travels from a far way place, I was able to guess the power of trees in passing the message. The bell sound made us solemn as there was a sense of piety in it. It is unknown if the sound was restricted only for the living ones, for I am pretty sure that even the sleeping bones are sensitive to the punctual bells. Evenings were special in the campus and as PG students we were in the campus at least till 8.pm and there were times when we used to touch the leaf filtered rays looking at the footprints of the day students.

There was a sit out in front of the centenary hall, just under a tree that could accommodate at least four persons. It was a raw, unembellished stone that was often hot with the day's heat. But still at the sun's fall, we used to sit to chat and smoke. Smoking was forbidden, but still guys loved to nicotinize themselves under the stars. The silent lights in the campus had a lot of message to us, and somehow let me acknowledge that I felt the burden of past wrestling me in the campus. Everything in the college was old, but learners were new. The light during the Christmas, the footprints on the walls, the dirty mosaics, the moaning fans, the grey windows were all bridging the past with the present. But the days slipped so fast, that I was not able to live the normal life even after the college got over. It was a literal dream and the harsh reality outside taunted me with its play. Five years were past stowing lots of emotions on our mental floor and till now we are unable to efface the imprints. Thus 'The American college' is a great place with great experience and the red buildings are reflections of the young blood that had flown with the time. I was so joyous then and I attribute all that I have today to my *Alma Mater*. The American College is as much a tourist spot as the Meenakshi Amman temple, and an air traveller would have wondered at the beauty of the spot that resembled on oasis with its intense green cover dotted occasionally with the red building and red sand. Great people breathed here and many more learn to breathe at this great spot.

FESTIVALS

Madurai as already stated, is more of a village than a city, it is a place that celebrates every festival with gusto and let me begin with the most popular festival in and around the temple city. At an age of ten, I was so excited when the *Festival of Lights* descended on the town. It was a great occasion and in 1980s, in Gandhi nagar, the festival started weeks before the actual date. Me and my brother purchase packets of crackers from a *Mathichiyam* shop that was literally a road side one. We were happy to get two types of crackers of which harmless *Cheenivedi* and *Olaivedi*[34] were in vogue. Though it was hardly ten rupees, we loved to get the packet and we used to burst it in a single stroke. It was in terrace did we burst the crackers and at times, the side shed where the car was parked was used by us. The pathway between gate and the car shed was reasonably a long one jammed between the compound wall and the residential building. A small fault like space was there on the residential part that had a door, and most of the times when the cricket was played, it was a habit for me and my brother to sit in the space. It was in this compound wall that most of the crackers were placed for bursting and we were very particular to get the papers on our side of the pathway. Our initial experiences with the crackers were such that my granny used to divide the crackers amongst me and my brother. We used to exhaust the whole stuff on the eve of *Diwali* itself and on the morning times all the decorative crackers would be exhausted that would leave us empty during evening and night of the festival day watching others burst the crackers.

---

34   A type of low profile crackers

Even though it was a short duration, Diwali holidays were special for people like me and I would feel the grip of the festive atmosphere on our home, with the new dresses arriving from the tailor shops and the sweet smell of Diwali delicacies floating from the kitchen. A lot of *Murukkus* and *Thattais*[35] were devoured by us with great rapidity, and the skies, the day before were usually dull and cold as every part of the town would be busy with a lot of movement and some lanes were dull with scarcity, but still there was a notable festival energy in the people's behaviour. I remember the heavy rains that hammered our celebrations at times. Once, there was a such a burst from the skies and I watched the close,slanting watery lines touching the buildings, lamp posts, roads, and trees in its own speed. But the next morning was not unpleasant to celebrate in a wet atmosphere. Usually, in boyhood days, I slept with the smell of crackers and my mother usually came late from the kitchen and woke me up an hour before the sun rise. I used to take bath and by five would take up the sparklers,while my grandpa used to try hard to wake up my uncle to light the crackers. He used to come in the laziest manner and with the match on his right hand and the crackers on the left used to ignite the red *Saravedi*[36] and throw it on the road from the first floor. The bursting sounds echoed all around as it was the first burst in my street. Gradually, every family member would get ready for a Puja followed by a sumptuous breakfast that was inconsequential for us. It was a time when TV was absent and the day was spent in chatting, and sometimes with the visit of few relatives from nearby places. It was always a practise in those days for nannies from my school to visit our homes to get the festival money. A lot of people knock the doors, of which the *Thavil*[37] people are ones, who used to play the music that would force us to drop few notes. The whole street was active

---

35   A typical diwalisavouries
36   A red fast bursting crackers
37   A tamil musical part of the Tamil culture

as many young and rich guys were competing with the each other in cracker bursting. A lot of sound pollution happens on that day with the dull smoke from the crackers used to waft slowly spreading the sweet smell on every object in the vicinity. The afternoons were a bit sad, as I felt the day was slipping out of my grasp and there was no more joy in the store. As expected the evening were dreary as my store of crackers were exhausted by then and I used to watch the cracker bursting events all around. Everywhere, the smoke of crackers would intrude and make us feel the power of *Diwali*. A day well begun often ends up in a sad dull way, with sleep touching us at an hour earlier than the usual time. Thus changes did happen like learning the art of bursting bigger crackers instead of confining ourselves to the small crackers. But more than the Diwali times, the very next day was even greater as I used to wake up a bit early and ken my eyes towards the road where the burnt papers of the crackers would be littered. It was an age that felt proud with the amount of papers that were spread in front of one's house. For this specific reason at a later time, I used to burst crackers like *Lakshmi vedi*[38], so that there are more papers in my part of the road. Thus, *Diwali* had always been a great time for me and my family, and for long, even after becoming a nuclear family, we never missed one another during the festive times. Every member of our extended family assembled at our residence, and the same procedure was followed except for the entry of the television that changed the dimension of our life. Pongal Celebrations it did not have any thrill. It was a bland festival, and in my boyhood times, we followed the dull protocol of praying in the court yard with the mud stones holding a couple of *Paanai*. The rice and *Sakkarai Pongal*[39] were getting boiled in the heat of dry palm leaves, and once the water brims to the top, a special Puja was performed to the sun, and there ends the *Pongal* celebrations. But the way in which we were forced to

---

38 A loud bursting crackers that delivers a lot of papers
39 A sweet rice prepared during Pongal celebrations

eat our lunch during the *Pongal* day was the toughest challenge, but I usually managed to taste all the vegetable recipes on the plantain leaf. The dull *Pongal*[40] celebrations became a thrill with the onset of TV channels as many programmes were aired that excited us. The *Pongal* days in the *Pasupathinagar* house was a joyous one, as we went out to see the competitions that were held all around. More than that, the feeling of togetherness in the family, made us really enjoy the occasion very much. As one walks through the muddy roads in my area, a lot of sugarcane leaves were scattered, and the movement of the cows painted in decorative manner gave a special kick, though I did not feel any special attraction towards the beauty of the place. But now as I lookback, I could feel the weight of the glory then.

Pongal was an abnormal festival, but the crowd and the movement on the roads and the togetherness of the family gave a boundless joy. There were many more celebrations in Madurai and most of the festivals were localized except for the *Chithrai* festival. The festival usually fell in the month of April and May, and often it began with a low key *Kodiyetram*[41] but gradually, it gained steam and in 1990s when we went in to the town, we felt the swelling crowd in places like *Simmakkal*. The *Pattabishekam*[42] was a part of the celebrations and it often happened in the evenings. The celestial marriage followed the *Pattabishekam*, though not immediately, and it was the day on which the whole Madurai was abuzz, for each and every resident felt a sense of joy. Once I was literally caught up in the *Goripalayam* bus stop and the crowd was so big, that I had to wait for more than two hours, before managing myself to enter a crowded bus with sticky bodies balancing one another with little space. In a few days from the celestial wedding, a greater event occurs with the *Lord Kazhalagar* sailing all the way from *Alagarkoil* with an intent to attend his sister's

---

40   A tamil harvest festival
41   A temple flag hoisting
42   A coronation ceremony

wedding. On reaching the outskirts, he comes to know about the completion of wedding formalities that enrages him and makes him enter the river *Vaigai*. It was a practice for my family to watch the happy *Alagar* near *Pudur*, and the whistle that often accompanies that entourage is a reminder of the Lord's entry. A huge crowd could be seen and people like me used to stand on the outer rims of the asphalt road to watch and worship the lord. Traditionally, he used to be decked in black, and there used to be a black band near his eyes. A mirror was set in front of him and whole town rejoices his entry. Individual houses on the pathway used to erect a *Pandal* for the lord to enter their gates. Every person in Madurai during the time would be speaking about the movement of the lord, and no one would ruin the chance of glancing at his face even once during the festival time. The heat and the joy, the crowd and the togetherness makes people enthused, and this is one festival that makes all the residents of Madurai a single entity.

Apart from the mega festivals, festival like *GanapatiChathurthi* and *Navaratri* too had its splendor. During the *vinayagarchathurthi* times, the roads in Madurai became congested, with a lot of vendors vying with one another to sell their clay wares. The *ArugamPul*[43] and few other flowers were sought after by the public and all these vendors were busy selling their items. I still remember the morning when I personally went to the *BB kulam* road to buy the clay *pillaiyar* and flowers. Though the crowd was a bit less as it was an early morning, still it confused me as I was unclear about the way in which I was supposed to take the clay *pillayar* home without breaking. Usually Madurai people were more passionate in celebrating the festivals than others, and the interest they exhibit in enjoying the *Navaratri* is a class apart.

Navaratri is one festival that made Madurai a highly interactive town with people moving with a constant word in their mouth. Once

---
43   A wild grass with medicinal properties

I did visit the temple, and the scene I witnessed was such a long queue and I walked along with my family for more than an hour to watch the grand *Kolu*[44]. It was irritating then to stand, but in reality gives good feeling to recall the experience. No town or city in TamilNadu celebrates the festival with such gusto like Madurai does. Every road had vendors who were selling puffed rice and flowers, with crowd spending money to make the celebrations a grand one. In my home, it was different as we had a Saraswati photo which was usually placed on the pyramidal arrangement of books. The books were swathed by a new saree and a plantain leaf was placed underneath the stool, on which the pens, pencils, boxes, sweet bananas and other fruitswere offered to the goddess of learning. In school days it was the happiest day as there was no need for me to touch my book, and I spent the whole day on Television.

But the very next morning was *Vijayadasami* and when my Grandfather was alive, he used to goad the women of the house to conduct the prayers at the earliest, and the books would be taken out for compulsory learning. It was a hard task, but we did not realize the joy of those festivals then. In a way, I lived mechanically without consciously enjoying the times. The evening of *Saraswati Puja* was special as we had a *puja* for our vehicles followed by a small ride with a lemon squeezed under the tyres. In 1990s, in *Pasupathinagar*, the festival was celebrated with great awe by the auto drivers. It is fair to mention the fact that the number of autos in that part of Madurai almost multiplied and during the Puja times they used to play songs through speakers, and in the evenings they perform a Puja after which they go for a fast ride. A lot of autos used to assemble near the main road bus stop, and there used to be a sort of rally which would be unacceptably fast. The honking of horn and the speed terrified the residents, but still it was partially a village that none could open their mouth.

---

44   Exhibition of dolls and images

The area as mentioned earlier has a small temple known to people as *Karupannaswamy* temple. In the earlier days when we settled there, it was a small temple with white pyramidal structure that was fenced with lots of spear at the back. A *hundial* was at the side and a *Vinayaga* was deeply seated looking to another side. There, a festival for this temple used to be held in the month of May or June. It was usually a three day function, and when we were in the main road of P&T nagar, it gave me a special thrill as it was a new experience. There used to be a *Molapari*[45] and the procession was interesting for cracker burst and the green saplings fresh out of the mud in the pot. A lot of women carried the pots and for few day before the festival actually starts, there used to be a folk recital at the *Pattimedu* village which had a *Mariamman* temple. The people used to increase the volume of the folk recital, and the *thanana* lines get repeated for umpteentimes. The whole village, irrespective of the gender, joins the procession and the residents generally watch the joy of the village life with a great glee. The highlight of the whole episode is the entertainment programme that followed in the evening. A small paddy field near the bus stop, that was barren in summer was used, a stage was erected at the farthest place and the audience were allowed to sit in front of the stage. Since it was a paddy field left barren, the ground was uneven, but I, my family alongwith our friends waited with mats and water bottles to watch the performances. The tiresome wait was irritable, but still the *Abinaya* dance programme used to be fantastic. The performers resembled the actors and actresses doing a scintillating choreography for the audience. Likewise, there used to be movies, and the emptiness that I felt then, while returning back to my home in the empty street was really tormenting. Most of the times, I had to knock and wake up my mother to enter, as my parents did not show much interest in these programmes after some years. I have always been captivated by the aura of the festivals, by the crowds, the smells,

---

45   A fresh grown sapling

and the liveliness. Every time the festival got over, we awaited the arrival of the next year.

Margazhi[46] is a special month for the Tamil people and it usually falls in December when temperature falls drastically due to the onset of winter. It is the time when a dull blanket of fog could be spotted in the circles of Madurai, and the paddy fields would reflect the greenness due to fog. The place where I stayed had a lot of fields once, and as mentioned earlier there was a canal that drifted the waters to the sleepy wintry fields. Religiously, it was a holy month for Hindus, and it is the period in which temples are opened up hours before the dawn. The villages spruced up the spiritual atmosphere by playing the spiritual songs even when sleep is pitched deep in our body. I have heard the *L.R.Easwari* songs that used to be played with a blare somewhere in Pattimedu. While preparing for the board exams. I felt a sense of reassurance when the songs were played. Though I seldom visit the temples during the *Margazhi* month, the songs and the charged up atmosphere had always enthralled me. At times, when I walk to the Karuppanasamy temple, on those occasion, I could see a lot of preparations being made by the people in the makeshift stone. It is a month that pulls everyone into the spiritual vortex. The songs of those days are deeply embedded in our minds and whenever we hear it, our memories turn back to those irretrievable past.

Madurai has lots of temples in the villages and there lots of villages in the peripheries. Often when I sit on my verandah during the summer nights when silence reigns, the smell of some night flower pinches the nostrils; from somewhere in some corner, songs and dialogues of movies do come to me all alone without much fuss. It gives a special feeling for people like me, for something disturbing was in the distant sounds, though the disturbance was the positive one. The feeling of oneness and the mental picture of the big tree,

---

46   A tamil holy month

the serial sets, the *Pandal*, the people crowded all around to watch the programmes – everything pops up in my mind.

But slowly things are changing at a rapid pace and the number of temple festivals is dwindling dramatically. Even more, the ban that has been imposed on the use of core speakers and the restrictions that has come into force regarding the volume has delivered a terrible blow. But these sweet experiences are really great and evergreen.

Aadi is another special occasion for Madurai people, though it does not have the same value for south as for the people of western Tamilnadu. It is a time when the small *Amman* temples become active with people buzzing around it with a specially prepared porridge for supply. As Fridays were very auspicious, special *Pujas* were performed and the weather in turn was special as the wind used to rock the trees unsetting and disturbing the sand that lie on the roads.

Festivals and celebrations are wonderful ways of making oneself happy as it fosters brotherhood and togetherness by bringing the whole village together. Though festival is celebrated by the whole town and some by the whole nation, nevertheless the joy that could be had through these togetherness is unimaginable. When joy is at its brim, it is tasteless, but when we are back into the future, it tempts us with the golden memories that winks from the rim to be drunk only with the eyes of the past.

PERSONS

It is not my intention to eulogize a person who has had a visible impression on us those days, but to remember them and to reflect the past to some extent that may visibly interest the readers. But who could be the first one who needs much focus, and the answer may be a bit personal, but certainly would be worthy reply by picking my grandfather Thiru. A.SUBRAMANIAN. He is still the most worthy 'hero' I have ever met in my life. A tall, gaunt personality with white hair combed behind, spectacled, unmoustached clean shaven face, long ears and ash marked forehead are some of the indelible features of this great man. He was a retired DRO with all the administrative acumen in him. For many years, I know him as one who used to sit in a comfortable yellow colored easy chair, with red handles and would be reading newspaper and books. It was always a practice for him to read a set of spiritual books and pictures before having breakfast. After the stipulated time, he spent most of his mornings in reading newspapers and in 1980's, when we were in Gandhi nagar, we purchased the Indian express newspapers. He used to count the news and words by ensconcing himself in an easy chair with a white dhoti and a full vest. The white curly hairs in his hand and the black Kasi threadare visible impressions in my mind. He was so commanding that I used to be in terror when he was there. Every time when the Marksheets came, I used to stand at the back of his chair to escape from his scoldings even though I was a good student. His confidence and the way he dealt with the officials was awesome, that made me a passive observant and fan. But during summer, me and my brother had a tough time as he was very particular that we were not supposed to go and play in the hot sun. But we were unrelenting and we used to wait till the hanging umbrella goes missing from its position in the hall. When it goes missing, it meant that my grandfather was out and we used to use the opportunity to run away from the house. He expected every one of us to work hard and it was a habit for us to discuss politics and cricket with him. His habit of listening to the 6.45am All India Radio news every morning is still fresh in my mind and the voice of Saroj Narayan swami is still audible. A lot of my uncle's friends used his help to join the Government Jobs then, as even in those days recommendations were part and parcel of the job recruitment. He enjoyed every festival with great vigor and loved to keep the flock together. In other words, he loved joint family, but days and years separated the set up to such an extent that isolation has become a hallmark of the familial system in India. I was under his command throughout 1980's and 90's, almost till he succumbed in the year 1998.

There was an old professor in 1980s, who was a retired Madura College professor with age bowing him down. But still with his hunch back, he would visit our home every evening to handover *The Hindu* newspaper and take away the *Indian Express* paper. He was a short frail man with partial baldness and unmoustached mien. In those times, old men avoided moustache and I have heard my grandfather asking his sons to remove their moustache. The professor used to wear a white dhoti and white shirt with very ordinary foot wear. His enthusiasm regarding politics is unmatched and he never failed to discuss it with my grandfather. Discussion on politics was a common thing in those times and people really had time to exchange views regarding the same. It was an era of Rajiv Gandhi and every time there used to be discussions regarding his policies. Televisions and newspapers were filled with the great leader's visits to different parts of India. I still remember the brown jeep self driven by him with Sonia ji by his side and we used to admire the couple for their simplicity and greatness.

Though all these things appeared in TV, naturally my family were great fans of the Gandhi and were firmly under the impression that none could rule India better than the dynasty. There were lots of rumblings in Tamil Nadu after the legendary M.G.Ramachandran passed with a wide political space for new aspirants. One point that recurred everywhere is the Sri Lankan problem. There were frequent bandhs and a large influx of Tamils from the island nation was a common thing. There were refugee constructions at the outskirts of every town and with the entry of IPKF, there were special radio programmes as well in Tiruchi All India Radio channel.

Another person who strikes my mind at this juncture is one Prof.Narasimhan, who was a stalwart in physics. He was my tuition teacher in 1990. He had a nice home that was neat and clean, and he requisitioned us to sit on the hall to write tests. The classes were generally taken in a small room that had reasonable number of chairs. He was not a strict man, but never failed to hurt the students hard by pointing out at their performances. I still remember him for his acoustics class that was exceptional and it has stuck to our minds so hard that it is difficult to erase. He used to touch upon politics during class times and never failed to mention the Sri Lankan issue that was hot. This great teacher, flickers in our memories even now and I still remember his slow walk, thick eye brows and slightly obese body.

One other person who was very much in the roll in 1980s was one Dr. Raja Gopal, who was one of the most popular child specialists. His hospital was near the Pandiyan hotel road and it was christened then as Bhooma hospital. It was a road that was largely deserted with scarce movement of vehicles and people. I do remember the days when my father took me to him quite often. It was a clinic that had a large tree, and an uneven pathway. The doctor's room was on the left corner after the entrance into the premises. A red cemented slab projected out of the parapet wall that allowed the waiting patients to sit. The physician was a staunch Aiyappa devotee and his fast speech and sharp diagnosis had often impressed me, though I knew not much in that age. He was a bespectacled man with simple dressing habits, and a white screen like stuff that was in the wall had caught my eyes in those days. Since it was 1980s, there was no such thing as Air conditioners and even the most famous doctors sat with windows open. He was very sincere that once sometime in late 1980s, my brother felt sick in the midnight and the doctor had to be urgently summoned. My father recounted that he walked from his home which was not far away and reached the hospital to treat my brother. It may appear quite simple in the paper, but such sincerity is something that is absent in the present era. By now, he should be significantly aged and with the hope that God would bless him, I wish to move to the next person in the list.

One interesting person whom I need to mention here is one who hailed from the borders of Tirunelveli district. His name was VenkatachalamThevar, and the white shirt and dhoti which he wore is still hanging in my eyes. He was my grandfather's right hand and often he used to visit our house in Gandhi nagar, and stay for a day or two before he returns back. He was not very tall, but was a strong man with well cropped hair and unmoustached mouth. His hush voice and immense respect he had for my grandfather could be gauged from his gestures and postures. His native place was in Deep South in the Tirunelveli-Tiruchendur stretch, popularity known as *Karungulam*. Seldom has there been any function in our home without the presence of this man. He is no more as he passed away in few years from my grandfather's demise. In today's world, it is hard to come across such strong relationship that is often spiced up with loyalty and truth.

Prof.D.Samuel Lawrence was not only my Professor, but also my guide and philosopher. He was not a tall man, but there was a majesty in him. He used to come in TVS Champ in those daysand post 1995 switched over to Kinetic Honda. As a teacher he was liberal, though at times extremely strict. He often dealt with prose, and I do remember his class that dealt with V.S.Naipaul's *India: A Wounded Civilization*. The Professor got too involved with the session, that he totally deviated from the actual content. Eventually, he returned back and sought pardon in his own inimitable way. His soft smile, gentle words and unassuming nature befriended him to many students. Once, a friend of mine smoked inside the lounge and it coincided with the arrival of the Professor. He got so furious that he locked the lounge instantly and took the key with him. In the following days, we were after him pleading, cajoling, falling at his feet and also fasting. His sturdy resolve finally dissolved and he returned the keys along with biscuits and tea. If at all I had fallen in anyone's feet quite often, it was in his feet. I genuinely miss those sweet days.

In Gandhi Nagar, the place where I spent my childhood and boy hood, there were various interesting boys all around. One guy, who had struck me and hangs firm in my memory wall is one Sridhar, just a year senior to me. A guy with brimming confidence and easy ways moved around with senior guys without much difficulty. In a way, he was a ring leader in 1980s. In early days of my boyhood, I used to watch him walk through the street with a shoulder bag – that was vague then-during evenings while returning from his school. He studied in Mahatma School, and his walk was highly disciplined with feet inverting inside. Few people have such walks and I have found them to be decisive and dominating. One fine evening I bluntly asked if I could join his cricketing team and he readily welcomed. From then on, we were quite close in games and he used to take us too many grounds in and around Madurai. He was a decent guy with strong business back up and never shied away from riding bikes and other two wheelers when we were pedaling our cycles. I am pretty sure that he was poor in studies, but a strong fan of KamalHasan.

During summer holidays, it was our habit to visit his home to play games like Ludo and other ones. On all occasions he exhibited raw courage and often when the cricket matches ended up with quarrel, he was at the forefront assuaging the tempers and at the same time exhibiting his readiness to resolve issues, with bravado. We used to watch the great Sharjah matches in his home as a group, and in every way he was a smart.

Days in school were slightly different as a lot of our mates are ones who had been with us for a reasonable number of years. In that way, I have a lot of friends, but a mention of few here would suffice. The boy was not very close to me, but was a Gujarati chatter box whose ease in moving with people had made me wonder at him. Manish was his name, whose tall, fair face coupled with shampooed hair and flat (alien) nose were feautures worth mentioning of him. He was very poor in studies, but had a wide circle of friends. An interesting aspect of the guy is that it is hard for anyone to see him sad. He was so active and talkative that went on with his harsh barbs, which eventually kept him at the top without any worry. Despite his *kutchi* background, the guy was proficient in usage of all bad words in Tamil, and never hesitated to use the same on Solemn occasions. An epicurean by nature, he ate and drank well to satiate his desires. Though smart (once), his tongue kept girls away from him, and he was hardly in love with any single girl, but at the same time ensured that others too are not loved by girls. If there was love somewhere, he used his verbal hoe to plough hard that eventually ruined a prospective relationship. Fortunately, he was also my college mate and many a times I was his pillion rider. Through him, I had access to the woman's college nearby my *Alma Mater*, and he used to blabber with one popular girl of our time, with me being a silent spectator. Though a lot could be said about him, it is prudent to confine his characterization to his "Joyous" life. Such persons are hard to see, and a North Indian managing all Tamil guys with ease and love is really a wonder.

In the year 1986, there were new admissions in our class and A.Shahul Hamid a tall strong guy sat with me. Though silent for some days, slowly I came to know about his Cricketing capabilities. He grew close to us and there was not a free hour without his burst of humour. I have laughed a lot owing to him and at times have got scoldings from the teachers too, for his jokes were silent. He was a born businessman and even in seventh standard, he effectively sold *Frooti* drink to the students. He was cool and never fussed about anything including the public examinations. He was a fitness freak and often visited the Gyms in Madurai. His liberalistic views and long term visions has vaulted him sky high that today, he is an unassuming VIP at the zenith of success.

He has helped a lot to the suffering lots and is almost akin to the modern day *Karnan*.

Prakash has been with me from the KG days. In schooldays he was a lean guy with brownish hair and exceptionally sharp in Mathematics. In our Primary days, his Lunch was usually late and I used to watch him and his brother tasting the crisp Chapathis along with sweets. He is another Great human known for his keen business abilities and philanthropic thoughts.

L.Rozario, an Anglo Indian teacher, was instrumental in shaping many young minds. I owe all my success to her. Her curly hair, the English dress, tipsy language and lavender perfume still roam in many middle aged minds. She was very sincere and taught us manners, politeness and hygiene. The development of Jain Vidyalaya was primarily due to her.

I am fortunate to have had met some of these great people who had a great say in my life in one or other way. I have learnt a lot from them in terms of values and behavior. All my Jain Vidyalaya mates are known for their politeness and other virtues. The very fact that not even a single student from this great school has had a criminal history till now vouches for its greatness.

FULL STOP

The present recordings are true from my heart, and it is more an outpouring than an artificial drawing up of the past. Madurai has been a part of our lives and even now bears a sentimental tag with it. Despite the mess and all the negative aspects, the town of Madurai would be loved by every individual who lives in it even for a while. We know not what the spirit is, but it is a moving spirit. There are different labels associated with the town of which the "Sleepless" tag is popular one. It either shows the active nature of the Madurai people or their restless minds. But for me, the love the people have towards one another and their attachment to the spots leaves them sleepless. It is a small turning back, and the readers are expected to discern the faults in a gracious manner.

Though a part of Madurai is still the same, a lot of churning had taken place with the movement of Time. Many old buildings have been crumbled, and traces of the past decades have been wiped out totally. The old silver coloured buses that were special in Madurai are no more, the rickshaws are entombed, the famous Tamukkam grounds are seeing new buildings, the old theatres are locked, the roadside tea shops are becoming bakeries, tricycles are replaced by minidor vans, the sodium vapor lamps are being replaced and the trains are getting modernized. Despite the sweep of time, the past lingers as people are more or less same. There are parts of Madurai that carry the indelible past in them; there are tea shops like Visalam Coffee bar still getting crowded in the mid mornings and late afternoons, there are still Lungi clad men walking here and there speaking the same innocent language, there are still half saree clad girls attending temple festivals and above all the Nayakar tradition of celebrating Chithrai festival is still alive. Personally, when politicians say that they want to transform Madurai into Singapore, I get annoyed. No, I want the same traditional Madurai. I want the same dirt and dust, the same smell and sweat, the same crowd and cycles. Madurai is a sentiment for me and I love to see it as it was in the past. It was peaceful, joyous and natural. Modernity is a farce, a clean gutter.

The happy days have melted and still we hold on to the empty cone. Madurai is not just a town, but a broadminded place that accommodates people without any religious or social affinity. It may appear to be a rude town, but people are more refined and well behaved than other places. Creativity has been its hallmark and the very fact that great people like Tms, Illayaraja, Vairamuthu, Bharathiraja, Sundar Pitchai and many more prominent ones hail from this very place is an attestation of its greatness. Times are changing and as modernity has usurped the life of people, the culture of the town has been under immense pressure to change. Fortunately, unlike other places, Madurai has more or less resisted changes. Corona has made a great dent on the social life of the people and it is very hard for the native people of Madurai to witness the demolition of the past in certain parts of the town. The construction in Tamukkam grounds is one sad fact that defies acceptance, but still life moves on and on. Many have come and many have gone, but Madurai as a town would live forever. Long Live Madurai!!

Made in the USA
Monee, IL
23 August 2021